Conversations at the Table

Father's Story

Marjut Karu

PublishAmerica
Baltimore

First printing

Cover art work: Alfred Karu, titled "Farewell" (1950)

ISBN: 1-4137-6298-0
PUBLISHED BY PUBLISHAMERICA, LLLP
www.publishamerica.com
Baltimore

Printed in the United States of America

This book is dedicated to my dear mother, Maire Karu.

Laughter and love have pulled us through.
Maire's influence and encouragement in the arts will not be forgotten.

ACKNOWLEDGEMENTS

Thank you to my husband, Tapani Nousiainen, for his support.

Thank you to my children, Markku and Katrina. Their kindness and love have always been blessings.

To all of the family who have shared in our time together, thank you. Special mention of the kindness of Rev. Paul Saar, Mr. Pantsa Paavola, Mr. Pentti Paavola, and to a hero, Mr. Pentti Taavitsainen in Finland.

And will I remember?
How?
The blueness of your eyes disappearing?
Silent chair sits empty where once – just
Now
you sat.
Staring eyes to eyes, blue and deep and lovely:
staring forever: the colour of memory.
And I am lost.
The edge falls off.

- Marjut Karu-Nousiainen

CONNECTING

Father, Father! I don't know where to begin now. Time and memories flow with tears streaming down my cheeks. A reflection in the window: it's me, late at night, at the table. A ghost? The window glass is black except for me, suspended in the light of the table lamp.

Suspended, with thoughts of present and past: breathing, breathing.

September 1999

Now the long rays of the sun were deeper, shadows lingered longer, as the days of summer were nearly over. It was September 12th. The phone rang. My sister Anne was on the other end. "Marjut? Hi, don't worry, but isi is in the hospital."

"What?" I was trembling. Impossible! Isi, my father, could not be sick! He had that nasty flu, which so many got at that birthday party - but he sounded so upbeat when I talked to him yesterday!

"Father drove himself to hospital; he had some sort of problem right in front of the doctor so he was sent from Napanee to Kingston by ambulance," Anne added.

I yelled, "We are leaving right now! I'll get Tapani."

How life can change in an instant. The fragile line that we balance on topples.

I called the doctor at Napanee who informed me that, if it was his father, he would feel better if he were in a bigger hospital. We rushed to Kingston that night, but felt that we would not be let in to see Father in the wee hours of the morning. We spent the night with Mother at my parents' lakeside home, getting up early to go to the hospital. Father had had a heart attack. Weakened by the dreadful flu,

9

he also had a little bit of pneumonia. As we rushed to his side, he looked fine, resting comfortably. We were relieved. He was in good hands, as Kingston General has a good cardiac unit with heart specialists. Father spent the week in hospital, endearing himself to the nurses with his humour and positive outlook. He was walking on the grounds of the hospital by the fifth day, and on the sixth, he was released.

Breathing a great sigh of relief, Tapani and I were apprised of Father's condition all week. Saturday morning, a week after Dad had had his first heart attack, we went to see him at home. Katrina came with us as she had missed pappa's 80th birthday, which had been in June. It was a gloriously sunny day, we were in high spirits, and so happy to see isi lying in his bed, watching television, with his happy grin. He was, as always, delighted to see us. We were a little worried when Father said that he had had a bad night of coughing. "If only this cough would go away, everything else is fine," said isi, as he got out of bed. "Time for a short walk!" he said. I went with him to the front of the cottage. We sat in the Muskoka chairs, and I kidded Dad about how much better the front looked now that some of the cedar hedge had been cut down, enabling us to see the lake much better. Just a few weeks ago, I had pruned a lot of the bushes and branches in the front of the property. I felt guilty, suddenly remembering how much Father wanted to help me with it, and I forbade him. Even so, he had picked up branches and taken them to the point, a favourite spot for almost forty years!

I looked at my father wearing his blue longjohns, with his paisley silk dressing gown on top. His legs were like sticks; he was so skinny. But he was happy, so full of plans for a great recovery. Take it easy; eat right.

We walked into the cottage. Mother was fussing about the pills for Father. As Mother has macular degeneration, I could not believe that she was giving my father his medicine – she peered at the pill bottles, holding them close to her eyes. How we take things for granted!

The sun was still bright, when we returned. Isi sat with us at the kitchen table. Suddenly, he looked very pasty, and said "I don't feel well." This was not our dad!

I called the emergency at Kingston General. "Hello! My father was released yesterday; he has been coughing all night; and now he says he is not feeling well. Shall we come there?" After too many minutes of waiting, we were told to come back to the hospital. Katrina helped her pappa get his pants on, his shirt. We wasted too much time. Isi sat in the front, Tapani drove. There was a red tractor in a farmer's field, and Father said that someone has a nice new tractor. He tried to make small talk, but we were all worried. This was to be Father's final trip along those beloved roads.

Night had fallen as we admitted Father – it took so long to get someone to see him! Tapani sat with isi in the emergency room while Mother, Katrina and I took turns going in to see how he was. Hours slipped by. I called Markku, our son. He sounded concerned. He was coming right away – he had the night off and didn't have to go in to work until the following evening. "No, you don't have to come; it's alright!" I protested. But he was adamant.

The hours ticked by; people came and went in the emergency room. Machines for chocolate bars and pop were constantly rattled. I paced back and forth. Markku arrived after midnight, going right in to see his grandfather. As he was a fourth year medical student, he was allowed in, and could also help us with assessments.

Still, no news of Father or his condition. We felt that he was okay, because no one was rushing with him.

At 1 a.m. we left, as we were told that Father would have to stay. We assumed that he would be comfortable.

Rushing back first thing in the morning, we went to find Father. He was in the critical care unit – with an oxygen mask on. I still see how he watched my expression as I looked at my hero. I skipped a beat and put on a smile, but am sure that Father caught the glimmer of fright in my eyes.

Well, Father had had another heart attack. But he was alright. Certainly he would be fine. We joked as we usually do, spent a little time with him and then started to search for a doctor. What exactly was the matter?

We were upset that Father had been released too early from the hospital. The stress of going home was not good, nor was the fact that he was coughing! That cough was a sign of heart failure! He had gone all night at home with it. We should have been told!

Clouds came into view, sombre and menacing. "Your father's condition is guarded," said the internist. Still, in our hopeful way, we were sure that isi would beat these problems. We would look after him, ensure that he would be fine. "There are a lot of things against him now," added the doctor.

We drove back to the cottage, Mother and I. We were in a stupor. I put up a good front. Mother was very hopeful. Surely things weren't so bad. We must pray, and do everything we can to help. We sat, bewildered, in the waiting rooms.

Father would see us come in, and he would wince. "Go home; enjoy yourselves," he remonstrated. I told him that I wasn't going to New York; I was postponing it until next year. Father looked at me with a smile and said, "We'll go together." I turned from him as tears poured down, soaking my sleeve. I pretended to be straightening up the food, which had been untouched. Things were unfocussed, blurred. The monitors were beeping and pumping; tubes were dripping, pouring needed nourishment and medication into Father's body. The heartbreak, the utter anguish! Mother and I paced the halls all day. What could we do?

So, Father lay in Kingston General, arms now swelling to stumps, his wedding ring of fifty-four years strangled in a new alarming shape. Chest that held me to him, rising and falling with difficulty.

Rushing, rushing. Mother, hurry, we must get to the hospital now – I have the porridge. I have the soup. This will help Father

Mother, I can't tell you yet what I know. Father is going to die; he is dying. He hasn't got a chance. Except for a miracle. Yes. We will hold on for a miracle.

Today we will hear good news.

How can this be? Everything in our lives precariously dangles on a precipice. Superman, my hero, strong and bold, laughing at obstacles in the way – that was Father. Don't go. Please come back!

Yes, I see that you are fighting, fighting to stay with us with your incredible determination. You won your fight for freedom, jumping into blackened nights and escaped from Siberian slave camps.

Now, bravely, we both look at each other. My eyes to yours, holding a secret. A sad final acknowledgement that these are the last of our days together.

Monitors blink, noisy, busy bustle of a hospital intensive care.

People whisk in and out, a certain detachment in demeanour. In a place where health is utmost, why does no one reach out in kindness? Cold white stares and demanding voices. "Mr. Karu, do you know how sick you are? Do you know? Do you want life support, do you want…?" Cruel. What? "Yes, life support, help. Help me," replies Father, not knowing the intendre.

"Why did that minister come and ask me about my will?" asks Father in a whisper. Alarm bells go off.

I turn to cry. So I lie: "Ministers are always coming and going around here; they visit a lot of the patients. I do not know why he would have asked you such a stupid question."

Father constantly cries, "Antibiotics!" He feels that this is what he needs; this will help him. Why are those doctors not helping?

Mother! You must come and smile, smile and do not look so terribly glum in front of Father! Your face has gone rigid with sadness.

Well, well, the doctor has come in to say something nice! Right, doctor?

My brother and I are taken into the hall. The doctor tells us that he is expecting Father to die within the next two days, if not the next few hours.

I run: run and scream. Shooting pains of shock and sadness and loss run through me. No! I cannot stand this; no, I will not accept this.

Father's second heart attack, along with pneumonia and a long-term kidney problem, have left him fragile. Surely this man can function with ten percent heart function. Like a wounded bird in captivity, he is in his cage of no escape.

But he fights instead. We fight together; we all fight. Taking turns, the family unites in battle.

Back in the room with false smile, I tell my father that I love him; please let me help.

"Okay, children, go home and take care of yourselves," says Father.

The nurse says, "You're wonderful."

Father replies, "I'm very wonderful – best on the market."

When the nurse asked whether the family was tiring him out, did he feel like he had to entertain? Father lifted his hands in his usual way with a bit of a shrug and smile. Two of his granddaughters kissed him and then Father turned to the nurse and said, "You too!"

Mother said to Father, "I miss you at home."

Father said, "Look at my picture!"

One morning, after a very bad night, with hardly any sleep, Father told the nurse, "When I get my sleep you should see what a nice guy I am." The nurses liked the man.

Father told me that he was glad that I was doing artwork, and that I would now have to continue with his work. He spoke of what a great artist Rembrandt was, about Monet. He told me that it wasn't important to be a great famous artist, but to be an honest one.

Then the voice ended. There was no strength. Medications flowed and machines pumped as we fussed and worried.

We brought in music though it was bittersweet.

We took turns sleeping on the cot next to the hospital bed. The family was all there. A bright wool Finnish blanket atop sterile sheets gave some colour and warmth to the scene.

We brought in some postcards of Father's work. Doctors, see, this man is not a number; he is a very good artist! See, we want him to get better!

Torture, torture, as we were forbidden from giving Father any liquids. He begged: "Tea! Tea!" It was unbelievable that we were denying him this simple thing. Hurting Father terribly, we did not give him what he pleaded for. This was painful and unreal. Instead, I insulted him with a pink sponge I was told to use to ease the pain of sores and dryness in the mouth. How can we live in this time in history, with such cruelty? No one should be dying in a hospital (or anywhere) with parched mouth. We were rather shocked and should have bought popsicles, ice cubes, anything! We failed.

Why did the staff not care about this, why?

I refused to let anyone say negative things in Father's room: no talk of death or dying. But was this right? Why did we not talk honestly?

Father hung on.

It was painful. We took turns so that Father was not alone. Alone at death must be a terrible loneliness. Or is everything blanked out at this point? Father's doctor was amazed that this patient hung on weeks more than he predicted.

We whispered in sad sentences.

The skies are painfully blue, bright and full of colour. The leaves are brilliantly showing off their Autumn coats. The clouds bounce about, leaving for other destinations. Father, do you still see the sky you loved to paint?

Are you a part of that sky? Certainly you must be; you are and always will be. I resented the beauty of the sky then.

We were not ready for you to leave. You stopped breathing and your beautiful wonderful eyes no longer saw.

Prayers were said, anger and sadness floated around you as we grappled with the truth. I limped away.

October 1999

Father lies in his coffin; I am in mine beside him. I lie in the box, head against the white shiny fabric. Stiff, afraid of breathing. Doctors peer in at me. I pretend I am dead. When the corridors are empty, I jump out of the box, running, running quickly. No one will find me; no one will know that I am alive. I must hide.

In the closet of my daughter's room, I hide with clothes and still air. I breathe silently, painfully. Katrina knows I am there; she is to tell no one. I awaken with a start.

September 2003

Words scrambled, thrown on the floor. Time has taken shape in memories where histories are repeated, retold.

Truths can be what we want to know. Stories highlighted by those of us who remain.

My father's remains are below me, in a container in the living room. He lives in the living room. Stupid thoughts, silly thoughts. Father would be amused.

I feel like I am flying off to a distant new land, one without a father, without the powerful humanistic person I knew. I am afraid that I will one day not feel so desperately at a loss without him. I will not honour him enough purely with the passage of time.

Mother sits clinging in the corner of her sofa, staring out at her lake, their lake. Emptiness envelops her like a heavy well-worn cloak. Yet the colours, forms and shapes Father painted fill the spaces. The walls are alive and he speaks to us still, though it is hard to understand that he will no longer enter the room, smiling, joking, putting his hand in the cookie jar. His eyes twinkle with warmth, holding us.

My story was going to be different. In my tale, no one died. All those we loved would not even get old! I had noticed, as a child, that others got old, but I would not. These things would elude me, would not touch me at all. The safety of fantasy in clouds! Clouds changed their identities, mostly dissipating into long lines of gathered showers.

In hindsight, I see the tragedy of the loss of precious time. But I did think, like some despotic leader, that I could control things, that there was always time.

Now, the sun is breaking through, and I hear my father's voice. I will continue. I wear his sweater when I am cold. Earthly remnants on my earthly body. Warming me as I travel to the past, to another sunny day.

Home Again...

Viljandi, Estonia, 1988

The sun is warm as we sit on the deck of the ship, enjoying each moment. My husband is reading, occasionally glancing up to look into the horizon or to talk to Markku or Katrina, our children. I look at my parents.

They are sitting tightly together across from me.

My "aiti" and "isi," people who I know, yet don't, journey to a place that I have only heard about.

To a place where I, as a young girl, would send letters. Letters received held another visual clue to the strange place stamped "Viljandi, E.S.S.R." though I always knew that it was really "Estonia" that should have been on those postmarks.

Letters from my "vana ema," my grandmother, were special. Pictures sent to Canada smiled at us, Grandmother staring with eyes like mine. The few photos of her showed a tiny woman, rather frail, with high cheek bones, wearing a scarf that tied around her neck, neatly. Her hands seemed strong, yet tender. She was an image in black and white, never colour. Never rounded, always staring with the same expression, in a captured moment. I would write to her, pressing flowers in the envelope. Choosing the flowers, just the perfect ones, was a special joy for me: chicory, the bluest ones I could find. Later I heard that the letters had been opened by suspicious minds of the day and Grandmother often did not get those flowers at all, my bouquets to her.

Gone now are the flowers, in letters pressed, addressed to a grandmother far away. Silent pictures, silent words still broke through all the longing she had.

Little children, what did we know of all the sadness in Father's eyes? When the news came that vana ema died, silently, the tears fell from Father's cheeks. Hopes of ever reuniting were gone. Father clung to his mother's memory from long ago. I never knew her but still I cried.

Silences through the years of growing up, Mother would sit in the corner chair at times, looking off into the distance, but not focusing on anything. Mother, why are you crying? Here, I'll bring you some flowers.

Mother's Day we snuck silently into the car, early in the morning: father and three children, off to the north, to the woods. The wet springy earth in early May held secrets we would find. With bent backs, we would search for special flowers. Don't trample on any tiny ones, warned Father. Be careful how you tread on the earth. We all gathered our treasures, then triumphantly got back into the car, excited that we would please Mother. We were conspirators for a happy cause. Arriving quietly, tip-toeing, we went into the kitchen and made batter for pancakes. I would, at eleven, be head cook. The delicacies would take forever to make. Later, we found out that Mother had been up for some time, waiting patiently. She always pretended to be asleep until the pancakes, coffee and arrangements of flowers, along with cards, homemade, would arrive. Anne, Jyri and I would hug Mother, like puppies vying for attention, almost spilling the plates on the bed.

Rituals, family stories, snippets of events from the past crowd my mind today, as the ship is making its way to Tallinn.

When we were young, we were told that we would never see any of our relatives in Estonia. Mother told me that we were not allowed to go there and the people inside were not allowed to come out. The Iron Curtain: was it really a curtain? How big was the curtain and how did it stay up? Where was the curtain, and what was behind the curtain? Was there torture behind the iron drape? Iron-willed, iron curtain.

What I envisioned was a wire. A barbed wire, enforcing the people to stay in. I imagined a long wire stretching like my tightrope at the cottage. But this one was barbed and dangerous, cutting and surrounding a whole country, going up and down hills, across rivers and lakes. People tried to get out, crawling in the night, digging holes, poking through the other side, only to get caught, sent to Siberia. Siberia was cold, a wasteland. There, people were freezing, starving into skeletons. Held captive, Mother told me. Many people, Father's friends too. Why?

Let's not talk about these things. These were dangerous topics; we might get caught; we could be sent to that place too, I thought.

So Estonia was an encased country. Encased in wire, forming a box with no openings. Occasionally, through the box, we would get those letters. Even these held a mystery, a sense of great achievement: they made their way out!

What did Grandmother sound like? Was my voice like hers? I pressed her picture with my fingers.

Father never talked about his past. We would get hints sometimes, when he would swing on the high bar, when he would joke with his friends. Do you remember? Not that it really interested me then. My own world of school, sports, friends, day-to-day living absorbed me.

There were times when my parents argued, late at night. Money, money, you spend too much; you come home too late; you don't understand. I would freeze, for fear. Sneaking into my sister's bed, I would hold onto her for safety. I would cover my ears with the blankets, warming myself against the cold sounds of the words.

Mother, Father, why are you so sad? So angry? Father never paints anymore; he is always at his business. He started another framing factory and we rarely see him. On Saturday afternoons he comes home and lies on the carpeted floor in the living room, with the bright sun warming him and filling him with strength.

Like clothing pushed to one side, not used again, the years passed.

New clothes, new styles, were front and centre. Rushing on, I gave little notice to the past. Clothes packed in boxes, given to Salvation Army: pieces of our history. No wonder people hang on to old ragged sweaters or dresses for decades. The memories have a shape, smell, style. Some of our precious clothes were kept. There is the tiny blue and red dress Mother sewed for me, which I wore when we left to come to Canada! I touch it, feeling the fragile white lace trimming, the scooped collar, the soft pleats at the front. A dress made for a little girl who was more interested in playing in the sandbox, or peeling the paint off her older brother's wooden car. Where were we going? On a big ship? Why?

Memories rush in, like unexpected white light, blinding the eyes for a moment, then fade. Grasping, grasping for a memory. What is it exactly that we did? What did he say, she say, we say, they say?

I said, "I do"; he said the same; we were married.

Time spinning and spinning, gathering momentum, we let go. Each of us in our own compartments, even those tiny little miracles born to me. Life holds a pattern; I see it now. Safe in my world, so far.

Extending out to others, often bossy, worrisome, I have not shed many characteristics of my childhood after all!

We bask in our children's warmth, reflecting love to and from them. We are blessed. Bobbing on the sea, waiting to dock in Tallinn, I wonder why the past is haunting me, suddenly.

My children would know my father in a completely different light. This older man would have the time to show my children interesting things, to play jokes on Grandmother, to laugh. This older man had slowly and painfully been shedding his history and past troubles. He had learned life's lessons well, coming up, like a joyous dolphin twirling on waves. Happiness had to be seized this moment. It made no sense to worry, finally, after all was said and done!

Now we are speeding towards strangers whose faces had only been black and white, except for Uncle Heino.

Dear Uncle Heino, my real uncle, Father's younger brother. In 1986 my parents invited him to visit us in Canada. As soon as I met him, I felt I had always known him. He was still very handsome, spoke softly in Estonian. Chain-smoking, in awe of all the wonders of the free world, he enjoyed every minute of his stay. Glad that I had retained my Estonian language, I heard of his life behind the Iron Curtain, of his wife and two children. I learned about my cousins Andres and Sirje.

Now, nearing Tallinn, that ancient city, I was first amazed at the cloud of smog layered on top of it, hanging like an old orange gauzy curtain. The ship was docking and we all ran out, stretching our necks, trying to see if our relatives were near. My heart was thumping in my throat as we finally were let out into the line of passengers, clearing through tough customs. Count every penny; list all your items. We were coming through! Through the Iron Curtain! It was invisible, but heavy nonetheless. Uneasily, we stopped and waited, picked up our loads of suitcases filled with presents. Stopped again, waiting. We were waves of motion and could feel the nervousness of others like us, straining to see loved ones.

Finally out, we saw Heino coming towards us. Everything was a blur. My children gave me comfort, as I held them to me. Then the front steps of a hotel, with an arrangement of all our Estonian relatives, with flowers, beaming. The grip of communist rule was still there.

We had to get special permission for our relatives to come up to our hotel rooms. We also knew that there were microphones in the rooms.

Once inside, we just looked at each other, everyone talking at once. We opened our suitcases, gladly giving gifts. Spilling out of bags and wrapping, our carefully thought-out items were admired. Heino's wife was lovely; I liked her immediately. I liked everyone! This was an incredible day. Father was walking around as if in a dream. Uncle Heino, you make me cry: why, why? I could not stop crying. At dinner, the streams of tears rolled out; I could not control myself. I was overwhelmed.

Long ago, I had heard about things. Long ago, I knew that I had people far away, who belonged to me. I connected and sat and sobbed. There was no simple explanation for this behaviour.

We made arrangements for the following day to visit our relatives in their home in Viljandi, Father's old house.

This required a special pass that would take a week to obtain. We only had three days! Speaking in English, my husband cajoled, paid extra and immediately we got help. A driver was ordered for us; he would also be our guard.

The following morning we left for Viljandi. Harri, our driver, would be watching us. We only had the day.

There are moments in our lives that are the jewels in priceless beauty and meaning: weddings, births of children, and this day.

As we approached Viljandi, we were all silent. Father told the driver where to go, remembering the streets of boyhood.

There it is! My, how it's changed! It used to have so much land around it....what bad shape it's in! Father was excited. We all got out, anxiously. The house was shabby, stucco, steps slanting to one side. We walked to the back of the house. There was a certain importance to this; we stood back and let Father go on. Father fixed his hands against the kitchen window, peering in. Was he thinking of his mother, his father, when he had last been there? Father knocked on the window.

Mother, I'm home! It's too late.

We visited in earnest, trying to inhale each moment as much as we could, to remember the paths of Father's childhood. Bright and dazzling was the Sunday that we spent together, exchanging our histories in one day. Warm was this time, as we walked through the old streets, recounting the past. Moments remembered with fragments blue in haze. Who were these people, Father's people, who built a country, then were caught as pawns of war games? Books could not tell the tale: it was lived and breathed in colour, right here.

We sat in the living room, eating lunch together. A coffee table was laden with bread, some meat, pickles and relishes, small cakes and cookies. How hungry we were!

Afterwards, we all walked to the old ruins and then to the swing bridge or Ripsild. This swing spans the lake at the edge of Viljandi.

My cousin's son came up to my father, wide-eyed. Is it true that you are the one I've heard about? You were the one who did stunts, handstands on the wire of the bridge?

The legend stood there, before him. Fifty years ago the man was known for his daring and charisma. Now, Father stood there smiling and remembering.

The bridge was truly a swinging bridge; it swayed as we walked on it. My cousins had to hold me, as I tottered slowly, afraid I'd slip through the huge holes of wired sides. I was not my father's daughter on that score!

Time stood still, as we walked to the graveyard, overgrown, neglected. Now, here was Grandmother, her flat gravestone flush against the ground, barely visible through weeds. We had brought her flowers. Grandmother, do you remember me? Did you get my chicories and daisies? I search for lifelines no longer there. I stare at all before me and cannot take it all in at once.

Where is Jaan, my grandfather? Why did we not hear from him? He had left Grandmother for another woman and things were never the same, we hear now. Our relatives whisper. What was it that we did not know? He is there in the graveyard too, in another area. Father's ties to his own father were broken.

The shadows of the trees swayed in the sunlight as we walked back through the main street of town. Time again had stood still it seemed. The village was not in vivid colour as I had thought it should be. Shades of brown, tones of grey, unpainted dwellings that were sadly neglected formed the real-life picture.

Almost a sepia print. The town I had now come to see, finally, was ironically muted in dull colours. The little square in the middle of town was overgrown with weeds, abandoned except for some bent figures, seated on the benches. No one looked anyone in the eye in this town. But we were certainly being watched. With our giant video camera, we stood out like blazing sirens.

A few soldiers marched past; we felt uneasy. Our relatives spoke in hushed tones, cursing the system and rulers under their breath. Entering the grocery store, my cousins came up to me. "Disgusting, isn't it? This is what is offered to us! We are rich in agriculture, in raising beef, but take a look at those glass jars!" Inside each of the big containers was a slab of meat, or really, of fat, floating in some liquid. I stared at the row of jars – with the ribbon of meat on the side of the white shiny fat. "You see, we have to supply Russia with our good products. How do you like our assortment of vegetables? Wilted carrots, some lettuce, lots of beets." At least it was all cheap; a loaf of bread cost the equivalent of our five cents.

Being talkative, I commented to a stranger that this was a lovely day. Taking my arm, cousin Sirje rushed up to me, nervously. "We don't openly speak to anyone here; we don't trust people. How can you be so free? We look over our shoulders; we are careful that we say and do the right things."

We walked on, enjoying our family, linking hands together, our happiness, shared, was tangible but fragile.

Back at the old house, filled with our laughter, we were together, as if in a dream. The tone became serious as we were told of life in this house in Estonia. Uncle said, "We play a great game of charades here. A survival game of disguise, while we despise. We know who to go to if we need some cream, who to go to if we need some special meat, like we got for you today. We work like robots. We don't really care if the quality of our work is good or bad; it's just the same to us. We get our weekly compensation, our pittance for showing up and doing our jobs. Aunt works in a dairy; I'm a graphic artist, drawing propaganda. What else could we do?"

My cousin had to join the Pioneers; she had to pretend that she believed all that was being said – how great the communist system was, how wonderful the great leaders were. Freedom was not an option. Yes, they longed for it, could almost taste it, could only hope for it. I was seeing that iron curtain as we spoke.

Some music was put on; we danced. One, two, three, one, two, three, swirling in the little room, we hung onto each other, looking into each other's eyes. Footsteps now dancing, the sun took us away!

Father was strange, very peculiar. Mother was annoyed. "He is not at all like himself! Marjut, go and find your father! He is wandering down the street like a little lost boy!" Yes, his silhouette to the sun, Father walked alone, lost in his own world.

I was also shocked at the primitive conditions of the house. The bathroom was only a toilet, rusty and ancient. A pull string ensured that it would be flushed. Toilet paper was a luxury and there was no sink. I walked to the tiny kitchen and washed my hands in the rusty old sink. No hot water. There was a sauna in the backyard but this, too, lacked any modern convenience and was dilapidated. What Canadian money could do to fix these things! My relatives had lived like this, while I had plenty at home. The contrast made me sad and also ashamed.

The clock struck five and we saw that Harri was still lurking in the garden, waiting to take us back. His engine was running.

Pictures were taken. Relatives with eyes like mine smiled and stared into the lens. These would be colour photos. We stood in front of the house. The shadows were long now as we lingered, hating to leave. At the last moment, our son took his new Finnish jacket off, handing it to his second cousin. Margus's eyes lit up and our hearts were filled with love. We climbed into the car, blinking as tears fell.

Through the glass windows we waved, looking behind us, until the car swerved sharply to the right and off we went back to Tallinn.

The train brought our relatives back to join us the next day and we walked along the cobbled ancient streets, looking in awe at the city built in 1200 A.D. It was now a run-down city with certain shops for the elite, the party favourites. Favours for the favourites.

Yet there was a burst of colour along the streets, dotted with people selling flowers and goods. Father took the gnarled and stained hand of one old lady who sat selling cornflowers, daisies and lilies. "Please may I hold your hand? It means a lot to me," said Father.

"My hand is not clean enough for you to hold, dear sir."

"But I would find it a great honour to hold your hand, madam." Looking at Father, her voice broke as she recounted her sad tale. All was lost to her: her husband was taken during the war, never to be seen again. Her only son died for the country, and she was alone. Her pension was not enough; she needed to sell flowers.

Later, Father painted her picture in pale blues, greys. Her

haunting and sad old face stares at us behind a bouquet of flowers.

In 1988, Estonia was breathing some first breaths of small liberties. Gorbachev had done much, paving the way for *perestroika*, for more freedom. The week that we arrived was signified by the fact that Estonia was once again allowed to raise its own flag. Flags that were waving, nation reclaiming, freedom speaks! Still vulnerable, sensitive and frightened, many did not dare to raise the flag of blue, black and white.

We walked along the streets and came to a wonderful sight. A small group of people were bunched together, holding an Estonian flag. It was raised carefully, slowly, fluttering in the wind against the bright blue sky. The full impact did not hit me until later.

Suddenly, Father broke away from us, ran across the street towards the group. Please, let me hold that flag up, please, dear sir. Father's hands clasped the pole tightly. He looked up, waved the flag back and forth. We could see our relatives looking on in disbelief, a little frightened. But I saw a man who had come full circle, back to a place that mattered. A place that had shaped him. Coming back to Canada, Father had a stroke a week later. Luckily he recovered just about everything, except that his memory had been lost, just a little. Was the trip back to Estonia too much for him? That accounted for his strange behaviour. He was probably in shock, not telling us how he really felt. Were things left unsaid, I wondered.

Father, tell me now, about your life, what you did, why you left Estonia? Then I can understand my own life, too. The silences, the looks of sadness in your eyes, in Mother's eyes...

1994 – Father Speaks

There is an uneasiness that settles in the house while we speak of the past, even today. Should certain things be left unsaid? Why dig up old sad memories? Unease still, of speaking about political facts. When are we ever safe?

For my father, the man who now sits across from me, tales of the past and of his life come with difficulty. I have a sense of urgency. I want to know about his life, to capture his history, linked to mine.

How can it be that he is already seventy-five years old? He looks better now than he did ten years ago after all the trouble. His grey hair is still wavy; he has a mischievous smile, and takes life much easier now. He laughs, enjoys jokes and making lots of fun. He is absolutely dedicated to Mother; I see it now so clearly. Yes, he does worry about her. He worries about his children, but the intensity of the worry is gone and he has learned to enjoy each day. He often tells me, "What's the sense in worrying? Stop worrying so much. Do your art. You can't change the world."

"Where did I learn to worry, learn to be so intense, Father?" We laugh.

The tape recorder is turned on. My father begins to walk back and forth in the kitchen, finally sits down, clears his throat. My mother sits at the far end of the table. Father begins.

"It's like this. Let's go back to 1919, to a time and place far away, to a free country, Estonia – a country that tasted freedom for only a very short time – from 1918 to 1939. During this brief respite from wars and repressions, Estonia strongly emerged as a country with its own unique culture, language, music, art. This was truly quite incredible, considering that the influences of so many other rulers had been so great.

"It was the year after independence from Russia, on the 8th of June, 1919, that a young woman named Anna gave birth in a small house in Kartsnavald, Estonia. Her first child, a boy, was born. All the village ladies had brought their cakes. It was a beautiful day with flowers and lilacs blooming. Everyone was happy, and the boy entered a world of hope and great expectations.

"The father, Jaan, was nearby. He was a shy man, slim and short, high cheek bones, and a head full of brown wavy hair. He was the head gardener for the big estate in Kartsnavald, an artistic man. The mother, petite, with sensitive mouth, and deep blue eyes, was musical, singing and playing the kantele. The young couple named their son Alfred Johannes.

"Life was dictated by nature, and life was simple. Rich fertile fields surrounded the little house, and Jaan left in the early mornings, beginning the work on the huge estate. But Jaan always wanted his own place, and also, he wanted to put to use his artistic talents, which he had learned....

"So, before the baby could walk, the family moved from the estate, and rented their own house while Jaan farmed the land for himself. Jaan was a very independent young man, and wanted to prove that he could make something of himself. The boy Alfred grew up in the country, surrounded by nature. He saw flowers, forests and animals. All this affected him very much. Life was gentle, held a certain pattern. The neighbours were kind; life was good.

"In 1922 the boy was taken out to the barn, and sat in the hay, listening as his mother screamed in the house. Hours later, the boy and his father went in, and there was a baby, a little girl. The parents named her Laine. But the young boy was not very interested in the baby. She cried a lot, and the boy had to stay indoors, keeping an eye on his sister while the parents worked in the fields. In those days, a piece of clean cloth was wrapped around sugar, and this was given to crying babies to keep them quiet. The boy offered this to the baby many, many times. But as the baby grew, he noticed that she was not very quick, and also she was very quiet.

"The boy had always been small and weak, and when he got the German measles, it could really have taken his life. But there was a country doctor who cured him. He still remembers when, after months spent in a darkened room, he was taken out for the first time and he saw the spring sun. He saw the spring flowers, smelled the fragrance of the earth. He loved nature, even from a young age.

"A great day remembered in the boy's life was when his father bought a horse, bringing it straight to the little boy to touch and stroke. This horse's name was Mira, a beautiful white mare. How the boy loved this animal! The horse followed the boy around like a dog.

"The boy remembers this also: when Mother got the horse and sleigh ready for a trip to visit Mother's sister, dear Aunt Kadri. Mother put in the warm blankets, with the horse in finery. The bells jingled when the horse pulled the sleigh through the snow. He can still see that picture. And then they arrived at the aunt's house. She had a very good character, very friendly. She had made pancakes and all kinds of wonderful food – the best she had to offer. The wooden house looked big, with a huge living room where the dining table was set with hand-woven linen tablecloth, foods filling the sparkling dishes. Oh, the smells of the baking of bread in the oven!

"Aunt always gave the little boy lots of goodies. He overheard the chatter of his mother and aunt, talking and laughing.

"This is where the young boy met other relatives, especially the uncle and older cousins, named Eeni and Alex. A strong friendship grew among these cousins. Eeni taught the young boy the ABC's, showing him the first letters needed for school.

"Then there was this story: now we'll still speak of this time. The little boy loved animals – always dogs and birds, all these he liked. He was given a dog who he named 'Palli.' He was white with black around the eyes and paws, a beautiful dog. The two got along very well. They slept together and were inseparable. The world of make-believe and adventure captivated the boy and his dog was his trusted friend.

"One day, the boy overheard the adults talking. They were going to move to a new place, this time to a town. They would be leaving in a few weeks' time. Much had to be done before everything was arranged. Well, the dog can't come to the town; there will be no place for it there, the adults were saying. The boy couldn't believe what he heard next: yes, the dog should be shot; it would be better! Running out of the house, the boy ran off with his Palli, and went into the forest to hide. No one was going to take his dog from him. The world was suddenly a dreadful place, a dangerous place. Together, they dug a hole in the earth, and made themselves a type of hut. They hid here. Darkness came and the boy was frightened, but he had his pal, and held him close. Hours passed in the night.

"Well, of course, the whole village was alerted that Alfred was missing so a search was started. The adults soon found the pair and promised that the dog wouldn't be shot. Neighbours took the dog as their own, but the separation of boy and dog was very painful.

"Believe it or not, the boy had a special tree and talked to it. Stroking it, he would also listen intently for it to talk back to him. He was certain that the special tree had a language especially for him. The landscape was very beautiful where they lived in the country.

"Town life! Viljandi was an incredibly big place for a small boy. The streets were big, with tall houses. The Viljandi Lake enhanced the scene, with wonderful hilly countryside surrounding it."

My tape recorder clicks, and now Father is starting to relax, remembering his childhood. He continues, changing into the first person singular, giving an indication that he had now become, in memory, that young boy. My father now seems to disappear into a fairy tale and I see him through the words spoken:

"We rented a house with how many rooms? Three rooms and a kitchen. For me then, it all appeared large, but the rooms were rather dark. At night, with the oil lamps lit, we would listen as Mother sang, laughing softly and playing with the baby. I built all kinds of things from wood pieces and twigs, arranging them on the floor. I still wished I had Palli, though.

"Viljandi, yes! Viljandi was also where a country boy saw for the first time a bicycle. Well, a country boy had come to the 'city' and saw that the neighbour's son had a bicycle. I got to know the boy right away and he taught me how to ride it. There I was, unable to sit on the seat as I was so small, but I managed to work the pedals just right, able to crank up and down as I steered down the street, the wind blowing in my face as I pedalled. I was fascinated with the bicycle, and wanted to ride it all the time. I always snuck the bicycle and charged off down the street with it. The boy's father caught me one day, yelling that Alfred had stolen his son's bike. I replied that I was only borrowing it temporarily. So that is the bicycle story. For a child, everything is big.

"When I was seven, my brother Heino was born. Now I was big brother to Laine and Heino. It took a while for Heino to be able to do anything so I continued with my exploring. Off I would go, as soon as Mother let me, to see what exciting things could be seen in town. I didn't like looking after the younger children at all.

"One day Mother and Father went to visit, and left me with Heino. He was sitting by this time, so I put him up on the table to watch me as I rocked on the wooden rocking horse. What a fine horse it was, too, complete with braided rope hair, and a finely painted face. As I was demonstrating my abilities, Heino fell off the table and hit his head on the floor, right on a knot that was protruding on the wooden floor. He screamed and held his breath. A huge lump appeared on his head and I was very frightened. I held him, and hoped he would not become retarded, which he didn't.

"The day came when Mother took me by the hand, put new trousers on me and said that now it was time to go to school. I would rather not; I was having fun at home, no need to take me off, Mother. Rules were rules, so then I went to school.

"'Why, you're no bigger than a flea!' shouted the older boys as I entered. To add to this insult, the teacher asked me the first day: 'Boy, how many lights are there on the ceiling?' I answered back in my country dialect: 'One, two, three, four…' and everyone started to laugh. Country boy! It was obvious that the country boy had a lot to learn.

"Sister Helju was born in 1928. She was nine years younger than me so by this time, as a nine-year-old, I was quite capable of looking after her when needed.

"The school days passed, and I enjoyed it. I had a history teacher who I liked a lot, and he liked me. Also, drawing was great. However, mathematics was a disaster. There was a problem because the teacher and I didn't get along. I made it through the years of school, but math remained a problem. Mother decided to make matters worse, from my viewpoint, as she sent me for math lessons in the summertime at the home of the teacher I did not like at all! Once, looking at the man, I told him. 'You don't know how to do math; how can you teach me?' Perhaps the man was fine and the fault was mine.

"The principal of the school was very nice. He lived close by and we usually went down the road to school at the same time. Catching up to him, I enjoyed his questions and soft-spoken manner. Walking beside him, I offered to carry his books, and so every day, as long as he was our principal, I had the honour of doing this. We were told that he was sick and, as I recall, he moved away. A good man.

"At this time, my father got the job as master set designer and builder for the Ukala Theatre in Viljandi.

"Mother interjects, 'Yes, the renowned Ukala Theatre.'

"Father continues: 'Yes, well, like I said, I grew up in the atmosphere of art and theatre. Here, at the theatre, I saw how sets were made. Picking up a paint brush, I started to help alongside the art decorator, Ott Kangelasti. He was a wonderful artist. Right away he said: "Boy, you have a great eye for colour."'

"I remember when I drew an old tree, and Kangelasti's brother Jaan, a graphic artist, came by one day.

"'How old are you?' he asked.

"'I'm nine,' I replied.

"'You have a great sense of colour, but you don't know what perspective is. I'll teach you.' So excellent lessons were given by the two artists. I learned a lot.

"Every time Jaan, (or "Checko" as we called him) came to town, he would come to see how I was doing, asking how many drawings I had done. 'You must make sure you go to art school,' said this wonderful man. Checko was a light that signalled to me that I should continue with art. Trying to please him, I diligently worked on my little pieces so that I could show them to him.

"Grandmother, Father's mother, lived nearby. I didn't really know much about her life. Where was her husband? All I saw was that she was very religious. She always went to church, sometimes twice a day. Of course she dragged me with her. Here, the minister asked me to draw religious themes. Of course this was of interest, but not the church, because I didn't understand what was being said. Also, the smell of the old ladies bothered a young boy. They would sit on the benches and the boy would feel sick. There was a reason for this. En route to church, the old ladies had to go to the bathroom and would stoop by the roadside, lifting their skirts. This the young boy witnessed, by telltale signs in the snow.

"In any case, the church-going did affect me in a special way, and the minister must have been wise to have noted my interest in art.

"I can still see Grandmother. She was small and fragile. She was the type who always read the Bible from morning till night. She held the Bible right up to her nose, as her sight was bad, and she didn't have glasses.

"Once she came to visit, and was given the guest bedroom. I snuck under the bed, and when she lay on it, I started shaking the bed vigourously. Grandmother screamed: 'The Devil's come into the house!' Poor Grandmother. I hid myself and she never really knew. But others in the family have since reminded me of how I scared poor Granny.

"But the lady had a kind heart, and when I cut my finger on a new pocket knife Father had given me, it was Granny who healed the deep wound. She wrapped a spider's web around the cut and was most attentive.

"For the summers I was taken to my aunt and uncle's place in the country because of my poor health. Uncle Alex was very nice, and he spent time with me. I once had a blood clot on the leg. It was awful, and very painful. It turned blue and throbbed. The country doctor was summoned, and he mixed a poultice, which was applied to the leg. Uncle sat beside me most of the night, holding my hand, kindly telling me that all would be well. The next morning, when I woke up, there was blood all over the bed – the clot had broken, and I began to heal. My leg looked like a stick. Soon I was able to walk. Aunt Kadri's food tasted wonderful, and I felt that I belonged. The farm was a wonderful place to be.

"At this time, too, I remember that President Patts was to drive by our country road at a certain time. All the country folk assembled to watch the President pass. What I remember is the car speeding by and a great cloud of dust. Summers at my aunt's house I will always remember. Here I learned to use a rifle, and to hunt, though I never took it up.

"In the fall it was back to school! One thing I also loved was music. I liked the violin. Before lessons could begin, the violin teacher tested me to see if I had a musical ear or any talent.

"I must have passed, as after this, Mother said: 'Now, son, I'll buy you a violin.' A great thing. So, a small quarter violin was bought for me. This was a wonderful event. I took lessons for three years and advanced quite well. I played with Evi Liivak. We had a concert together in Viljandi. Evi became a well-known violinist. Perhaps I, too, would have done so as well. Perhaps.

"But what happened was that, after a cold winter, my health failed again. I was taken to the doctor and he told me that I had to go to a sanatorium, where sick children were sent to recuperate. I didn't want to go! To make matters worse, Father came to my room as I was practicing the violin one day, and told me that I had to leave the violin behind; I had to rest at the sanatorium. No, Father, violin is everything to me! I even walked around, with a special glove on my left hand to protect it from the cold, so that I could play continually. The violin was also handled with extreme care, wrapped specially to protect it, even though I had a case for it. I always rehearsed and played that violin. The violin and I were now inseparable. But I was forced to go away. I hated to go.

"I remember the moment when I laid down the violin. I put it slowly into the red plush case and closed the lid. I thought: 'I will never again play the violin,' as tears rolled down my cheeks. I buried my music then.

"Father noticed, and said, 'You must become a strong healthy man, and then in the fall you can continue the violin – now your health must be looked after.' I had practiced on the violin every day, and was obsessed. I did play well. I was very angry and upset that my violin playing was taken away, and that all people ever said about me was that I was small and weak. I was twelve years old at this point. A few simple words: 'you must leave your violin behind' shattered me.

"When I got to the sanatorium, I decided to start training so that

I would become physically strong. No more weak Alfred! I dreamed that I would become a great athlete, a gymnast. I ran every day and exercised. Fantastic training! Secretly I would run and train, after our usual daily outings. There was a great trail encircling the building, and I could easily run around many times. Exercising became my new obsession. It is odd that I was allowed to run and do physical exercise, yet violin playing had been forbidden. I didn't understand this at all.

"So when I returned home in the fall, I didn't look at the violin, but went straight to the gymnasium and trained in gymnastics. I felt that I had been betrayed, somehow, by the violin. It hadn't made me strong and healthy. But you know, I have deeply regretted the mistake of putting the violin down!"

As Father speaks, Mother tries to keep quiet, which is not the easiest thing for her. Now she interjects: "But tell also that you painted then as well."

Father ignores this, just grunts towards her. She is distracting his thought.

"What I remember when I came home in the Fall was that my father had bought himself a new bicycle. We were told not to touch it. Specifically: 'Alfred, you are not allowed to touch this bike!' Well, I sure looked at this shiny wonder and decided to take a ride with it anyway. As usually happens with forbidden things, something bad happens…I rode off to the sports track and drove very fast round and round the track. Someone suddenly came along with his bike, and bump, we collided. I flew over the handle bars onto the ground. The other fellow was knocked down too. First, what I saw was that the front of the bike was now shaped in an eight. I felt sick. The bruises and scrapes were nothing. I hauled the broken bike home and placed it in its spot.

Soon Father arrived home. I went out to greet him, preparing myself for punishment. I could see Father looking at me, then the bike, and back at me. I said to him, 'I'll fix the bike. I took it and broke it.'

"Father replied, 'Where are you going to get the money?'

"Ashamed of my behaviour, I knew that I had to prove to Father that I would pay for my sin. I silently went inside. Mother looked at me: 'Oh, dear, you have gotten into mischief again. Come and have some supper. You'll work something out.'

"Well, I knew the owners of the movie theatre in town, and went to them and asked if I could get a job painting theatre ads. This had to be done at nights, after the movie was over, because the new ad for the next movie had to be ready by the next day. It took just about the whole night to paint."

"In the old days," adds Mother, "they didn't have ads like they do now – ads were painted by hand on cardboard and displayed outside of the theatre. Dad was then just thirteen years old."

Father continues: "So, from this job I got money, and listen, I bought the parts to fix the bike. Then my father said to me: 'I wouldn't have believed it, that my son would have done this. But you will become a man, you kept your word.' Luckily, my friend's father owned the sporting goods store so I was able to get some good deals with their help.

"Those humorous things of childhood! Well, the pancake story I certainly remember! This was when I was about thirteen. One evening, Mother and Father said that they were going out to the theatre (where Father worked). I urged them along, saying that I would take care of everything at home. 'Yes, yes, go on, have fun!'

"I shut the door, and looked at Heino, Helju, and Laine. I decided to make pancakes for all the children. I got about ten eggs and all the other ingredients, making a huge batter. Helju kept adding the flour; she was almost white from the powder. Big brother was showing off his great culinary talents. We had just finished lighting the fire for the stove, when Heino shouted, 'Mom and Dad are coming back!' I looked out the window, and sure enough, coming down the street were Father and Mother. Why did they come back so soon? With incredible speed we cleaned up and I hid the batter on the top shelf over the oven, positioning myself strategically in front of it. 'Be quiet, you kids; don't say anything,' I warned. My parents walked in. It looked like they had had an argument, as Mother left the room as soon as she came in, not speaking. Father sat down in his chair and started to read the newspaper, but his head was facing the stove. The children sat down casually. Then, something started to come down the sides of the wall, dripping onto the stove. The batter was oozing down like a huge wave. Slowly it dribbled down. All that baking powder sure was working!

"Father looked up, and started looking at the scene for some time and then asked: 'What is this? What's coming down?'

"I confessed. 'Well, it's pancake batter and we hid it because we thought you'd be angry.'

"Mother came back into the kitchen and exclaimed, 'Oh, my, you children have really made a lot of batter!' Then Mother made us all lots of tasty pancakes. Father laughed later, so much that his stomach shook.

"Well, yes, when I was young, the film *Tarzan* was the rage and of course all the young boys wanted to be like Tarzan. A group of us began to play Tarzan ourselves. We went to the park and literally swung from the tree branches. I was known as Tarzan – still am to this day – by old friends. It is true that I had no fear and loved adventure and sports.

"When I was about fourteen, I also wanted to make a sailboat for use on the lake when it froze. I had a blacksmith weld together the body and runners of the sailboat, but we needed a sail. Mother had lovely white sheets in the linen closet, and I started to eye them. What great sails they would make for my boat! Every day I thought about ways of making a sail, and knew where the perfect material lay. Finally, I stole the sheets and had a lady sew them to fit as a sail. This was all wonderful, but soon I started to feel badly about taking Mother's sheets. I remember Father coming to the lake to 'see how Mother's sheets were flying.' What speed my wonderful ice boat had! It was the only one in Viljandi.

"Skiing was another great pastime for me. One winter day, after spending most of my time skiing, I reluctantly had to get home; there were chores to be done. Later, I decided that I just had to get back to try some ski jumping from a rather high hill, Uuveski Hill, on the side of town. It was getting a little dark, but off I went alone, the great skier. It had been snowing for days, and there were huge snow drifts on the sides of the hill. The snow piled up many metres. I was practicing a technique called cross-jumping, where the skis are a little crossed during flight. Off I went, flying in the air, and suddenly landed, and was stuck right up to my neck in the snow. My whole body was plugged in solidly. I panicked – how was I to get out? My skis were like anchors underneath. No one was around, and I knew I had to get out as fast as possible. I began to dig around my arms, freeing first one arm, then burrowing down, so that I could unleash one ski. The foot came free, and then I set to work digging out the other leg, releasing the ski. Luckily this worked, and it was some time before I could dig myself out. Truthfully, I did get a little scared, as by the time I got out it was pitch dark. I left the skis in the snow but retrieved them the next day.

"At school, I recall a story that I wrote and read to the class. It was like this: 'On a nice winter day, a boy wanted to go skiing, but he had no skis. He remembered that his father had some planks, and so went and made skis from the planks. He carved them, and got straps, and was ready to go and test the skis. But the skis would not slide, they needed to be greased. So the boy snuck into the house, took his mother's soap, and greased the skis with this. Again, the boy tried the skis and this time they really worked! They slid very, very well, and you wouldn't believe how the suds and bubbles followed as the boy skied down the hill.' Everyone in the class laughed. I think I liked to be a bit of a clown.

"Always trying new things, I decided that it would be fun to do some handstands on something a little more daring than the ground. There is a swing bridge (Ripsild) in Viljandi that crosses the river. It had thick wire for the sides. I jumped up on the wire, which was about ten metres above the gorge, and did a handstand on the wire. There I was, having a grand time, balancing on the thin wire. I had no fear. People stopped dead in their tracks, frightened that if they moved, I could fall. People watched but it didn't bother me, because I was so well trained at this time."

Here, Mother interjects: "Yes, you remember the bridge, don't you, Marjut?"

"Yes, but let's get back now, let Father talk..."

"In Viljandi, there was a sports club and I was a member. The coach there wanted to train me for the Olympic team for the next Olympics (Berlin). There was a fitness craze at the time and it was very important for young people. By this time my health was excellent and indeed; I was asked to be on the Estonian Olympic team. Training began in earnest. But my Olympic dream was not to be

"During this time, drawing and art were in my blood. The Kangelasti brothers taught me the basics and foundations of how to draw – light and shade, though I didn't understand everything at the time. Patiently, the brothers kept teaching me. I had been drawing, using charcoal and pencils. I remember my first oil paints. An actress at the Ukala Theatre gave me this wonderful gift. I was so happy. Rushing home, I got a piece of cardboard and used a twig as a paintbrush. I painted a picture of a winter forest and an old hut, with a dog and fox on the ground. The texture was quite nice, using the twig. It was very hard to get a real artist's brush then – there were no such shops in little Viljandi.

"Life was great. I worked relentlessly on gymnastics and physical training and also on developing my art. The years passed. I was young and in good condition.

"Gymnastic training was then enhanced by a new passion of mine – to learn the high wire. I had seen a film about this, and decided that I, too, could learn this. I read books, and every day I practiced balance. Before long, I was getting up on a high bar, doing simple stunts at first. Then, after much practice, I could stand on my head. Also, another trick was to balance on a ladder that was on the swinging wire. I would slowly climb up the ladder while balancing on the wire. Once on top, I would put my left foot out, swinging slowly on the trapeze. Nothing scared me; I knew I could do these things. Training was the key to success.

"In the summer of 1937, I was offered a job in Parnu, to exhibit my gymnastic skills. This was at the seaside resort there – a well-known and expensive resort. I entertained there for a few weeks. I worked on the trapeze – no safety net. The trapeze moved; it was a swinging trapeze. The wire was about fifteen metres from the ground. There was a postcard made of me, showing some of the stunts. I was known as 'Alfredo Original.'

"Boy, was I paid well for this! One Swedish woman had red roses for me every night, and followed me around, but I was so stand-offish and aloof to all that. During the days, as I walked along the beach, people stepped aside and clapped their hands. What a great feeling, putting to use my abilities, with people applauding.

"Magda Soodor, who was an actress, and involved with the Ukala Theatre (she had been my singing coach, which hadn't worked out too well) had come to one of my performances and she told me later that she had fainted watching me perform, high up on the tiny bar, with no safety net below.

"For me, there was a sense of security, strength in my life. I trained hard, led a Spartan life. No humbug, no cigarettes, no alcohol, no dancing. At the dance halls, there was bad air, so that was not good for me. Just pure sport. At the time, I was one of Estonia's best gymnasts.

"Also, I made some money doing art work. Believe it or not, I made women's shoes from wood. These went well. Oh, boy, I made money! Using a special tool, I engraved the designs into the wooden shoes using a special burning tool.

Dad's trusty bicycle became the power behind the homemade sanding machine. Unfortunately, the machine was off-balance, so when Helju and Heino would pedal the bike to get the machine going, the vibration was incredible. The whole house shook! Father arrived home one day and laughed that soon the house would move off the property, it shook so much! But the shoes were nice, and if we would have had proper machines, we would have been able to make more shoes.

"Also, I engraved designs for cigarette boxes and the covers for photo albums. I had told my parents that I wanted to go to art school, and also to train for the Olympics. All seemed possible. Who was to know that clouds were gathering, that things would never be safe and secure?"

As the young sister, Helju, was Father's little favourite, the older brother taught her how to train. She had no fear, performing many athletic stunts with him. She remembers the balancing act they performed, where Alfred was on a trapeze, holding onto the bar with one foot in a loop, while he lay parallel in the air. She then climbed the pole and slowly Alfred grabbed her one foot with his mouth (an apparatus was in his mouth) – she then did exactly the same – she swung from his mouth, perfectly parallel in the air. It was an artistically beautiful and balanced act. She was about nine at the time. They performed in a big bandshell in a park in Viljandi, and also travelled to Tallinn.

Aunt recounts that she loved to perform in front of people, didn't care much about the training. But if she had an audience, that was just fine!

Alfred was a good brother and always took his little sister along. He even built a car for Helju – a wonderful wooden car with wheels that she could sit in and drive!

It really was a wonderful time and Aunt Helju's character, too, would be needed in the future to get her out of all kinds of conditions. Her path would lead her to many parts of the world, from Denmark to Argentina and finally to her favourite country, Canada.

But now we turn back the pages to the picture of a young man in his prime. Alfred basked in the promise of the future...

*"Alfredo Original" — Alfred's postcard, as trapeze artist,
Estonia, 1937*

"In June 1938, on a cool and rainy day, I arrived home late. Mother met me at the door. A special letter had arrived for me. I remember that day well. 'Alfred Karu, you have been conscripted into the Estonian army.' I felt odd, unhappy and unsettled. My life changed forever. I was 19 years old. Mother took me aside, and said, 'Well, now that you are going into the army you'll become a man.' She took me to the reporting officer in Viljandi. Looking around, I saw military men, the sharpness of all that is military. Signing the papers, I was put in the Sakkala partisan battalion. This was not a bad place at all, because there was a farm with crops. The food was excellent.

"The new recruits entered into this stage with confidence and unconcern. This was going to be another form of an education. The army never interested me. I hate war and killing, but I was forced to go. I had wanted to go to art school – not the army, but the time dictated otherwise. The dreams all stopped there – in the army.

"Well, I had a reputation already as a gymnast, so I was given a special section to go to. My commanding officer was Lieutenant Oidermaa, and he looked after me well. We were a part of the machine gun battalion. We young people didn't understand politics much and so our morale was indifferent.

"I had been in the army about six months, when one day everything changed: we were shocked to hear that now the Russians had come into Estonia! This was the Fall of 1939.

"While we were in our barracks, events were taking place that we had no control over. We heard that the Russians were approaching: we became worried, defensive. Our morale dramatically changed. We slept a few nights on benches, with our rifles ready in case there was an attack. We were ready to fight at any moment. It was a catastrophe. But what chance did small Estonia have? Russia was so big and powerful. We had no say. We heard that General Laidoner was imprisoned and that President Patts had been taken to Russia. At night, we patrolled the area on the roof tops. Lieutenant Oedermaa and I sat and cried like little children, because we knew we had witnessed the last steps of our freedom.

"It wasn't long before we were ordered to leave. We were put on a train and taken into the country where there was an old estate. The Russians were following at our heels, taking over the headquarters and barracks.

"The politruk came and spewed out communist propaganda. There were Estonians who became Communists, so we really couldn't tell who to trust.

"Well, I was commanded to go to Elva Kotka's headquarters near Tartu. They had an officers' training school here. I went to the officers' area where the commissar was, saluted and bowed to him. I had to say that I was honoured to now serve in the Russian army. Imagine! I looked at the small man with the enormous ego. What was he like as a human being? Without that uniform? Anyway, I spoke: 'I don't in any way want to hurt your feelings, but I don't want to be put into this training, because that would mean an extra five years in the army. I would like to be a regular soldier, as I am an artist, and would like to pursue this.'

"The commandant stared at me. He was furious, looking at me in disbelief. He pounded his fist on the table and shouted, 'This type of talk I have never heard – that someone should state their wishes – they don't want to train here when they have been given such an opportunity!' The powerful man was so angry, I realized that if I spoke another word, I would have had to face the army tribunal. Nothing helped. I had to go to officers' school.

"Captain Tarm was the school's head officer and later we had Lieutenant Riipalu, who was to become a hero in the war, a very good man.

"Officers' school was educational. We were taught discipline, respect for one another. This was quite an educational system, organized for the Estonian officer. As the new rulers knew I was a good gymnast, they ordered me to teach physical education to the whole Elva regiment. I said it would be hard to teach Russians as I didn't speak the language. The response was that I would learn Russian. So, I made up a program. As instructor, I had fun in a way, because I could train myself and had to demonstrate how to do gymnastics and teach the boys and officers.

"Yes, but one day I was told to go to Varska training camp, sixty kilometres away in the southern part of Estonia. There were some big manoeuvres – we marched there by foot, through forests, fields, marshland. We marched and marched. It was completely barren here. Somehow, the world spun past. I felt I was living in a bad dream. Surely, soon this nonsense would stop, and I would be able to continue with gymnastic training and art school!

"I looked down at my uniform, my new identity. My friends, my countrymen, were marching, all of us Estonian, except for those commanding. I had an overwhelming sense of loss, a feeling that I was nothing because the Russians had taken my homeland away from me. Even my own Estonian uniform was taken away and I was given a ridiculous uniform to wear. When I got the uniform, it was very big, with a long-sleeved shirt. I'm a small man, so it looked funny – I hammed it up and everyone laughed at me. It wasn't long before I was given a uniform that fit. That was the Russian uniform. Well, even in times of trial, I also had to laugh.

"All this I remember too, when at the camp they held the May Day parade. Then I was told to paint a portrait of Stalin for the ceremonies, to be hung in the hall. It was a big celebration and of course Father Stalin's picture had to be displayed. I had the time off to paint, and was given all the supplies. But I told the officers that I'd paint at night because during the day there was too much noise and commotion.

"So I painted a portrait of Stalin – quite big. The night before the big event, I hung it on the wall and draped the portrait with a cloth, to be unveiled at the festivities. But listen, at three o'clock in the morning I had a devilish thought! I snuck over to my friend, shook him up from his sleep. Listen, I have a great idea, come with me! We snuck into the kitchen. I got a large knife from the drawer, then we quietly crept into the huge hall, lifted the cloth that covered the painting, and I stuck the knife in Stalin's throat. A nice touch to the painting! I would have been shot if the Russians would have seen me do this! My goodness! But off I went, back to bed, feeling pretty good about myself.

"The morning went by. We were kept busy with preparations. In the afternoon, the big moment came. There stood the new leaders, the proud Russians, lined up smartly. The commandant, with much pomp, then unveiled the painting. Complete silence. The knife glistened on the throat. I was there, and of course exclaimed, in shock, that this was awful! Then the commissar started shouting 'sabotage, sabotage!'

"I was questioned immediately. Did I know who could have done this? I knew nothing. My portrait was ruined; I was very upset!

"The interrogation lasted two weeks. No one came forward, and I was not suspected. But it was difficult, because my friend knew, and I was always worried that he would tell. I was afraid of this all the time. But he never said anything. I did tell him that, if he told, then there would be one less person in this world – me.

"Otherwise, at first we didn't know how to be afraid of the Russians because we didn't know their system at all. But later, we started to understand, and became very uneasy when boys started disappearing: boys who didn't know how to keep their mouths shut, or whose parents were wealthy or upper class. These boys they wanted to get rid of.

"Varska camp was typical, where soldiers were taught army techniques, war tactics. But here, something strange happened. Our Estonian officers were told one night to assemble together, that they had to be sent to special training. All they needed were their toothbrushes and a towel. These officers no one saw again. Except, history tells us, that these officers were all shot to death in a forest near Riga. The Estonian army's best men.

"And who gave away the names of the best Estonian officers? An Estonian communist who knew how to speak Estonian and Russian well. His name was Kaanis – he made a list and gave it to the Russians. A traitor.

"One Sunday morning we were ordered to line up, and were told that the war had ended. Germany had taken over. This was June 1941.

"Now we know that events named Barbarossa changed the course of Estonia.

"A mother's love stands out for me still. My cousin Eeni, who was dear Aunt Kadri's son, became a Communist. But when the Germans came he was imprisoned for political reasons in Tallinn. Mother told me that Aunt knocked on our door one day, saying that she had missed the train, but was going to see Eeni. She had a bundle slung across her shoulder, in which she had packed food for her dear son. She decided to walk all the way to Tallinn. Yes, a mother's love. Her other son, Alex, was not a Communist. Politics were tearing families apart.

"War. It is a horrible thing. We Estonians felt at the time that something good may yet happen now that the Germans had taken over. At least we would get rid of the Russians. But this was another big betrayal.

"So here we were, never knowing what was to happen. Of course, the Russians were in a panic and we were taken back to Elva by foot. Here, all the Estonian officers and soldiers were given the Russian uniforms to wear, while the Russians put on Estonian uniforms – our best parade uniforms. The Russians were in a panic; there was complete disarray. The victors of one day were captives the next.

"When we marched, the Russians mixed with the Estonians. However, we Estonians had rifles but no ammunition, so for anyone who tried to defect, it was useless. We were being used as pawns, as decoys. Also, along the sides, the Russians patrolled, ready to shoot anyone who tried to escape.

"Awful. As we marched, more poor Russian farm boys arrived, meeting up with us. They didn't know how to read or write, didn't know how to use a rifle – they had come from somewhere, perhaps the Caucasus. Imagine how we felt. These boys didn't have shoes on their feet – but had rubber from car tires wrapped with rope – here were their shoes. Many were Mongolians. I was given forty of these Russians. I didn't know how to speak much Russian, except for some commands, but was put into the machine gun battalion to train these boys. They didn't know at all what a machine gun was. Completely uneducated, poor boys.

"We were forced to march to Voru, then south to Petseri, and into

Russia. As we left my homeland, a brilliant red sunset – a huge circular orange ball – made me want to weep. Perhaps I did. We had a very long march, hundreds of kilometres lasting many weeks. Hunger, we knew hunger.

"Before we knew it, the German bombs were hitting, and the Elva regiment was completely scattered in panic near the town of Porhov. There was no chance to march with just my group. I wanted to pull the Russians by the nose. I had hoped that during an air raid, with everything in chaos, no one would know where anyone was and then I could double back in all the confusion, and turn back to Estonia. But everywhere, there were Russians. The long march to where? For what?

"I remember a moment like this: we arrived at an estate, and a Russian soldier captured a chicken, twisted the head off, plucked the feathers while forty-one men watched. What would happen? But the Russian boy was kind-hearted, cut up the chicken in tiny pieces, so that everyone got a bite.

"Yes, those Russian times. We searched for the rest of our regiment because by this time we were all dispersed. It was chaos. Truthfully, I wanted desperately to get lost on purpose. But for every two Estonians, there were forty Russians.

"As we marched, I remember at one point we had a horse that pulled the cart with the machine guns. The wheels at the back broke, so we put logs on the back, Indian-style (travois). The poor horse. I felt sick to see the starved horse's neck raw, bleeding, with bones sticking out. I remember that horse; it would bury it's head under my arms. It was bleeding by the haunches, where the leather straps were. I put rag cloth there. What sad eyes the poor animal had.

I befriended a young man named Suhoff, who was a young Russian engineer. He gave history classes about Marx-Engels and communism. He had to do this. When we were alone together, walking, we talked of many things. We could have been friends, that's for sure. Unfortunately, he was mortally wounded, and before he died, he asked me to go and see his sister in Moscow to give her his greetings.

"The hunger was always there. We marched, slept, marched, often hanging onto the sides of the cart. Once, I woke up, half under water, but I hadn't even felt it, as I was so dead-tired. Such a waste of time for a young man – for anyone. The innocence! The lost youth. We knew by now that people by the thousands were taken in the night to Siberia. Families separated immediately. Intelligentsia, army officers, were the first to go, of course. We Estonians had nothing to fight with.

"But luck seemed to be with me, in many cases. For example, one night I had gone to speak to Lieutenant Oedermaa, and when I came back, a bomb had hit where I should have been. Another time, during a fierce attack, the cannons, grenades and air raids were blasting all around us. I heard a grenade come down, automatically dropped and covered up. But just beside me, my friend met his end. Half his head was blown off.

"A colourful snapshot of what I saw in Russia stays in my mind. Near Narva, which is on the other side of Lake Peipus, there was flat land, wheat growing, rich land. But no one looked after it. No roads, just rutted paths. The Russian dwellings, one hundred and fifty to two hundred years old! Log houses with thatched roofs. Under the same roof lived the people, the animals, the pigs. The heating system was this: people lived on the floor above the animals, as the animals would heat the house. No fire wood. In the spring, the thatch from the roof would be used to feed the cows, sheep or pigs, whatever cattle the people had. When I looked at the people it was like looking back a hundred years. They were dressed in ragged old clothes, string holding up their pants. No newspapers, they couldn't read.

"Once, I went to ask for some water at a house. A woman came out, was very accommodating. I looked at the cup the poor woman brought out to me – it was cracked and filthy, with a layer of dirt on top of the water. So I filled my hat with the water from their well and drank from that. This was Stalin's communist system – people reduced to such squalor!

"Having strayed from my regiment, I had hoped to double-back and return to Estonia. I lay down and slept under a tree, in the cold.

Suddenly I was awakened, and as I opened my eyes, a Russian officer mounted on a white horse was standing over me. 'Who are you? What are you doing here?' I was taken, along with the others, to the front lines.

"Along the way, we saw a hill full of dead soldiers. The distances we travelled were enormous. We marched north, the Russians trying to keep the Germans from gaining any ground.

"Reaching Kno, the place was completely burned down. Here, the Russians reorganized against the Germans. Arriving at night, it was a horrible scene. I had the machine guns, and went to a barn to try to sleep while the boys dug trenches, ready for battle. Trying to get comfortable, I touched a cold hand – a dead hand. When I got used to the darkness of the barn, I could see that all around me were dead bodies…I went out to the trenches.

"At about 3 a.m. I saw how the Germans were preparing for fighting, red and white flares were going off. Then suddenly, bombs, grenades, rockets hit everywhere. The earth was shaking. A major attack. The Germans ran towards us. Luckily we had dug the trenches. Beside me, a young man lay mortally wounded. He screamed 'maduska, maduska!' before he died.

"In all this chaos, Kaanin our traitor arrived. 'Now we go back – we'll withdraw,' said he. We had no intention of retreating, as we wanted to be captured by the Germans. Kaanin was despised; he was the traitor who had given the names of so many fine Estonian boys who were never seen again. Justice must have been served, as Kaanin was shot. No one there mourned his death.

"At 8 a.m. we surrendered, waving white underwear. Germans turned their machine guns and shot at the Russians. Now we were handed over to the Germans to help fight for Estonia's freedom!

German rule!

Another prison camp, this time in Pihkva. Again, no food, hunger. We were dirty and cold. The autumn was unusually cold that year. We did not know what was happening in other areas, but learned that the Red Army held out against the Germans and Operation Barbarossa failed by December 1941, though a new offensive by

Hitler's troops was mounted in the spring.

"One day, I began to dig a hole right near the fence. I dug so that I got my hand to come out on the other side of the fence – through the dirt. My side of the fence had some shrubbery so I was hidden. My prank was to get my hand out to the other side and wave it about – and sure enough, a loud scream was soon heard as a lady passed by and saw an arm coming out of the ground waving! I laughed – but to others it looked macabre – like someone in the grave with an arm coming out.

"Again, we were moved out. We were put on a train and thought that we were at last going to be set free in Tallinn, but the train passed the capital, passed out of Estonia into Latvia.

"New orders. My half of the camp was to go to Riga and the other half to Germany to work in the mines. We later heard that the conditions in the mines were awful, as the harsh conditions and starvation bloated the poor men's bodies. When some boys returned they fell and split open. The water retention in the bodies did this. It was truly awful.

"My section of the camp in Riga was not as bad as that of the Russians. These boys were truly starving. People starving crave protein, and so the boys took the shirts off their backs and ate the lice. They were full of lice. I picture them now, eating the lice with their teeth, huge eyes staring out.

"We Estonians were housed in the corner of the camp, near a relatively busy road, where the civilians did business and walked. I figured that we could get some attention. I told the boys that every night at exactly 8 p.m., we should sing Estonian songs. We sang pretty well, almost like a choir. People gathered near our building on the other side of the wall. The following evening as we sang, a wonderful thing happened: bread was being lifted over the barbed wire, lifted over to us. We were very happy! The bread of human kindness. However, the Germans did not appreciate our concerts so we were ordered to stop.

"But we were all very hungry, so something new had to be tried. I polished my shoes and requested permission to be presented to the commandant. 'Could we go to town to buy food with the money we have gathered? We have rubles.' I actually got permission.

"The next day a group of us went to town and got food. The sense of freedom, even a little, was uplifting. We bought sausages, bread, butter. For two weeks we were allowed to do this but then a new commandant arrived.

"Once again, I decided to ask for permission to go and buy food, and was taken to the new chap. He wore shiny boots, a pince-nez and held a whip, enjoying thrashing the whip around. His face was arrogant and mean. I pleaded that we would cut down their food bills if we could go and buy food to supplement what we were getting at the camp. This commandant looked at me for a long time, then shouted, 'Damn Estonian, get out!' I was whipped. I felt only rage. We were nothing, just a nuisance to the Germans. So again we tasted hunger.

"One day, though, some kind-hearted people gave the boys a pig and raisins. We boiled half the pig in water, with raisins in it. The boys ate and ate, being utterly famished. A dangerous thing to do, I cautioned the boys. But hunger eats away and, once food is given, it is hard to stop, as hunger is so deep. The next morning there were long lines to the latrine, and one boy died from eating too much on an empty stomach – he simply burst. I didn't eat any of the pig. It was a big mistake, eating too much, too fast.

"From one day to the next, we didn't know what was going to happen to us. The Germans ordered us to go and remove logs from the river, but I told an officer that we couldn't work as we were too hungry. Soon the officer returned and we all did get some bread.

"A sad thing happened here as well. We had been questioned all the time by the Germans, if any of us were Jewish. There was a very nice Jewish boy, who I befriended. We stuck together, and I was horrified, when one day, he was taken. Someone must have told, I am sure of it. Nowhere is safe.

"We stayed at this camp in Riga about one and a half months, when once again we were moved. Do you think anyone told us where we were going? No, we were like livestock.

"Niital, in southern Latvia, held out a better time. Here we got good food and three cigarettes a day though I did not smoke. We were told that we would be doing farm work. So off we were escorted to the town square, like slaves. I stood there, rather stupidly, when a man, who was also small, approached me. 'Do you know anything about farming?'

"'No, but I will learn if you teach me,' I replied in broken Russian. Who was this man? What was he like?

"Papers were signed and soon I sat at the back of a trim buggy. Off we went along the dirt roads, with fields stretching on both sides. We arrived at a lovely, clean farmhouse. The farmer's wife greeted me warmly and offered me a delicious meal. Why, she was like my own mother, I thought. I was well cared for, had my own room. This was a peaceful time for me, and was a respite from the army, the detainment camps and constant fear. The farm turned out to be a pleasant place.

"Working hard to please the owners, I also learned a lot. One job given to me was to build a fence of posts along the property. This I did with extreme precision. When I had finished, the farmer called his neighbours to come and see what his 'boy' had accomplished. The fence was very straight; you never did see such a straight fence!

"Ha! And then there were big fields, which needed to be ploughed. This was something I had never done as well, but two horses pulled, and soon I was getting the hang of it. I figured that if I marked certain lines and followed these, I would have a well-ploughed field using a geometric pattern. I created a lovely pattern on the fields, something quite original and unusual. Once again, the farmer called the neighbours to come and see my handiwork.

"In August, it was time to butcher the pig. 'Here, go and kill the pig,' said the farmer, as he handed me a huge knife.

"'I cannot kill the animal,' I replied.

"The farmer urged: 'Well, come along then, and help me hold the pig down.'

"'Sorry, I just can't do it.' I really could not watch this kind of thing. So the farmer butchered the pig himself. As to eating the pork,

I simply could not do this either.

"When I had arrived at the farm, I was weak from hunger. One day we had to go to the mill to pick up the flour. I was told to carry the one hundred kilogram sack down the stairs and to the cart. Trying to lift the weight, I failed, and the sack fell down the steps, bursting open as it landed. The kind-hearted farmer ran in, exclaimed, 'Oh dear, oh dear, I see you can't lift that kind of weight!' (me the great gymnast). Then we cleaned up and got another sack together, taking it home. It would have been wonderful to talk more with the farmer, but we spoke rudimentary Russian to each other, as I didn't know any Latvian, and the farmer didn't speak Estonian.

"All this time, I had not been allowed to write to my parents. I did write at night, but tore up the letters, fearing that I could endanger my family in some way if I wrote. They didn't know where I was. I also knew nothing of what was happening back at home.

"The neighbouring farms also had Estonian boys as hired hands and we would meet Sunday nights. One Sunday we got the good news that we could go home again! This was in September 1941.

"As I said goodbye to my newly-acquired friends, there was sadness too. The farmer and his wife had become quite close to me, and asked now if I could stay with them, be their son. The couple had been very good to me. But I had to get back home, back to my own family, feeling that things were looking good.

"However, things weren't to turn out at all as I had hoped. For the moment, though, hope surfaced again and I was free. Except, I was forced to sign my name to a document stating that I would always obey the Germans. There was no recourse.

"As I travelled back to my own country, I waited in anticipation. What exactly had been happening? The train back to Estonia held no clues. Were my parents safe?

"Finally, I made my way home to Viljandi. It is an evening I shall always treasure. It was smoggy that autumn evening, when I went searching for my family. I went to the theatre, as my parents lived above it. But a big section of the theatre had been burned down. I asked someone where my parents were; what had happened to them.

I was told they were now staying nearby in a little house. It turned out to be a pretty house, with flowers in the garden. I knocked on the door. Mother knew. She knew immediately, and cried, 'Alfred is home!' She knew the way I knocked that it was me. Dear Mother, how I missed you! Hello, Father! Hi, kids! I'm back! What's cooking?

"There was warmth once again being near my family. I brought home a carton of cigarettes. I had never smoked in my life before, had been against it. But I had lost my faith in humans, had seen the immorality of men. I had learned that the value of humans is nothing. I gave my father half the carton of cigarettes and told him, 'Father, now I'm going to smoke.'

"On a happier note, I remember how good it felt when I strolled, later that evening, out to the local restaurant, wearing a fine suit and smoking cigarettes."

As my father pauses, I wonder about how the passage of time weakens memories and often brings only things we wish to remember to the fore. I will realize years later, that Father has deliberately erased a part of his story – during the year of 1942. But now back to what Father continues with...

"Remember the piece of paper I had to sign, stating that I would obey the Germans? Well, how I got out of the German army is another thing. The Germans saw that they would lose to the Russians, and so Estonians were taken to Poland.

"The Germans wanted to send me to the frontier, but I then had a scheme. I studied medical books for some health problem that doctors could not pinpoint. I pretended that I couldn't walk, had an examination and, sure enough, failed my medical. Dr. Riipalu, an Estonian doctor, helped, got papers showing that I was not fit for the army, was indeed so sick that I wasn't well enough to make the trip to Tallinn (from where the boys were being sent to Poland). I was released from the German army.

"Soon at home again, I organized a gala of singing, theatre and gymnastics, a wonderful evening of entertainment. Of course, this had to be cleared by the Germans, who required that there be German content. But it was all very skillfully full of Estonian patriotism. Here, I staged my gymnastics. Sick that I was!

"My skills were put to use again, when I took a job in a circus in Riga. Here, the height of the trapeze was about thirty feet from the ground – no net under me. I performed here for two weeks, and you see, I got good money, which I needed for my future plans. Unbelievable!

"But time was running out. My charade was soon found out and I was ordered to Tallinn anyway. The doctor had a sealed envelope, which I had to take to Toompaa, Tallinn, the German commander's headquarters. The note read: 'Alfred Karu, fully well. Can be sent to Poland.'

"Luckily, I had friends here, so I asked for two weeks' leave. I had to go home. This was granted.

"So time and options were now limited. In Tallinn, I started to organize for my departure, my escape. Where? To Finland.

"There was a strong underground at the time and one had to be extremely careful, and speak only to the right people. If you didn't, as some of my friends found out – that was the end of the line

"I only had a few days to get things in order, but it was urgent that I get back home to Viljandi, to bid farewell to my family.

"My dear mother put sandwiches in my pocket. Crying, she hugged me tightly. Father hugged me too, giving me money, attached to my clothing with a safety pin. I couldn't tell my parents my exact plans as I knew they would be interrogated, and best that they didn't know all. And indeed, a while later, the Germans arrived at my parents' door, demanding to know where Alfred was. He had not appeared back at German headquarters. Heino witnessed this.

"I was never to see my parents again.

"The plan to get to Finland was very complicated. The danger was in who to trust. Luckily, I met my childhood friend in Tallinn, who I trusted. He told me about the possibility of escaping. My friend and I stayed in a rented room for a few days, keeping a very low profile. My friend had 'papers' showing he was an electrician in case he was questioned. But I had nothing. The steps began. I should visit a certain silversmith and order a cup with two handles. Entering the shop filled with ornate silver, I met a tall slim man and asked if I could order a cup. 'Yes, certainly, your order should be ready next day. Come at 7 p.m.'

"Arriving the next evening, not trusting anyone and shaking inside, I entered the shop again with my friend. The man greeted us quickly, motioned for us to follow him. We were led out the back door, and the man pointed towards the fence. I knew what I had to do. Quickly I climbed over the high solid fence and landed on the other side. My friend did the same. We found about nine other boys huddled together in the dark, very quiet. No one said a word. We didn't have long to wait. A truck drove in, full of furniture, except that in the middle, there was room for the men to hide. All of us climbed in and a tarp was placed on top. From the outside, it appeared as though the truck was just carrying old furniture. The truck driver knew the areas of German patrol and avoided them. From Tallinn it was a one-hour trip and then we smelled the sea air. Soon, we were driven to an old barn in the middle of a forest. We were afraid. In the total darkness, we hoped and kept still. No one knew where we were. We wondered if now the Germans would come. We could feel the tension even in the dark: all of us were silent.

"I had a grenade ready just in case...Suddenly, an old lady appeared, carrying a broom. 'Boys, follow me,' she said. We silently walked to the sea shore and here there was a small shack. 'Now you wait here.' The woman was gone.

"We all had money with us, for it cost each of us two thousand deutsche marks to get to Finland. This was a great deal of money. A man arrived after what seemed an eternity. He carried a gun and satchel. He took all our money. Suddenly we started to get worried that maybe we had been tricked. But we could go nowhere, so continued to wait. Then an old man arrived and he told us that we had to wait a while longer, a boat was coming from Finland.

"A while later, the man came back. He cried: 'Now – run! Get into the boat!' We made it, trembling. It was a good boat, a Finnish sea patrol boat, with a Finnish driver. A tarp hid us. We had only our knapsacks with us.

"The boat that October evening, 1943, smelled. I was very seasick and vomited into the driver's hat. Keeping a sense of humour, when asked by the driver who had done this, I replied that I didn't know! But my mind was really spinning. I remember that I wore my good suit. The trip across lasted four hours.

"How many others were stealing across to freedom? Hundreds of Estonians fled their country using small boats that took them to either Finland or Sweden. Families bundled up together reached the shores of safer places.

"Our boat docked at Helsinki harbour. The Finnish police greeted us and drove us to Jollas, which was where the Estonian refugees were. We were well cared for here. Some people decided to leave for Sweden immediately. There was no pressure to join the Finnish army; it was all free will, but many of us wanted to join. We young men were very patriotic and wanted to fight for Finland's freedom and, of course, for Estonia's honour. All was lost at home now. Without hesitation, I joined the Finnish army.

"We, the new recruits, were taken to the Helsinki Stadium where the Olympics were held, and here I was given yet another uniform, the Finnish one. I didn't want to tell the authorities that I had been an officer in the Russian army, as I had fiercely rejected this and had been forced to do this. So I didn't tell.

"Three weeks later, line up! We were on our way by train to Taavetti. I went into some more military training in Purho. It was ironic that I was now in my fourth army – me, who hated the military!

"Here I was, in a new country. Three months after arriving here, fate would lead me to an interesting person.

"One Saturday night in February, a friend of mine asked me to go with him to a cafe nearby, for a beer."

At this point, Mother interjects "Now Fredi, don't twist the story. There was no beer; we drank 'korviketta.' Also, it was a Sunday – the

13th of February, 1944."

"Yes, well, I didn't want to go at all," says Father. But my friend insisted," Father mischievously looks at Mother.

"But anyway, we did go. We skied about eight kilometres to the cafe, put our skis on the outside wall and entered. We sat down and drank some korviketta. I looked around, and noticed that at another table sat two girls. They looked rather pretty, both of them. I wondered which one I would go and talk to, when I noticed that one of the girls had very beautiful blue eyes and she smiled so nicely at me. Politely I went to the table, bowed, and asked in German: 'Do you speak German? Would you allow us to sit with you?'

"'Yes' was the reply. We somehow got along in broken languages.

"I taught the ladies a funny match-stick game where I always won. The four of us talked, and then I asked if I could see the young lady, Maire, home. 'Of course, of course, young gentleman!' replied Maire."

Father is relishing this, adding touches. Mother interjects with a big smile "It wasn't like that at all! I did not allow you to escort me home that night!"

"All right, but I was so delighted when such a good-natured person spoke to me. I did say that though I could not see her home, I hoped to be permitted next time."

Father continues, warming up: "My friend and I returned to our barracks, and I forgot the whole thing. It had just been an evening of fun. But, next day, a telephone call came, then a postcard, even love letters!"

Mother is now annoyed at the story being told incorrectly. "Fredi, you are twisting this completely! I did not call you right away!"

"Aha," says Father. "Maire did chase me. I have a witness, Hannes Oja. Oh, yes, he remembers all the calls. At any rate, the two girls made arrangements for another meeting the following Sunday.

Sure, I hastily skied to meet Maire again. There she was, waiting for me, her eyes big and blue."

"What else?" says Maire, in disbelief.

Father is young again. "I accompanied Maire back to her aunt's house."

"Now the truth," says Mother. "It was a long time between the first and second meeting – and I did not phone you, you phoned me."

Now we are all having fun with this. "Sure, Mom, for you it seemed a very long time! What is the truth? Did you fall in love with Father the first time you saw him?"

"No. My friend and I actually felt very sorry for those boys. They talked to us about how they escaped, their lives and their families. Our first language was German. Father spoke Finnish slightly, and I didn't understand Estonian. My first thoughts of Alfred were, well, I can't say that I fell in love with him then, but somehow he was so sympathetic, understanding and interesting. I was curious about him and had a great interest in the Estonian situation. It was like a spark in my heart. We didn't really know about the Estonians, except through the papers. That first night, after meeting the men, Senja and I spoke of how we felt about the Estonians, and how they had had to suffer. No homeland, nothing. I believe I gave Alfred my home phone number, so he could call me."

"No, no! You called me!" responds Father.

Ignoring this, Mother continues: "No, I did not give any phone number, I was not in the habit of giving strangers my phone number. I know what I did. I did send him a postcard, with greetings from Hamina. Then he called me."

"But, but, how did I know how to call?" insists Father.

"I don't remember how Father got my number," replies Mother, gruffly.

However they had their second meeting. Father walked Mother to her aunt's home, and then Father adds, "Yes, and she kissed me in the snow!"

"No way!" cries Mother. "We sat at my aunt's house, on the fence outside, talking."

I am inclined to believe Father. At any rate, Father says that he told Mother then, that "in three months I will come to know you better!" Alfred knew already that he was going to marry this girl.

It turned out that that Estonian boys were entitled to a vacation in March so Mother started to look for Finnish households that would be interested in billeting some of them. Also, she asked her parents if Alfred could come to her house and spend the week. Alfred had said that he could get some coffee. When Mother's mother heard this, she was delighted. It would be fine if Alfred wanted to visit. After all, coffee, real coffee?

Mother adds now, feeling a little put out: "Well, it wasn't love at first sight anyway!"

Father goes on: "My feelings at first were her eyes. From one's eyes you see into the soul. I saw that this was a good woman, only her lifestyle was wrong! Just kidding! She chased boys too much! Ha, ha."

"Now don't be like that!" huffs Mother.

"Anyhow, I did see something good in her character," continues Father. "I had been in love a few times before, in Estonia."

And now I must interject again, to elaborate on the reason why Father had left out a part of his tale. The gap in the story between 1942 and 1943 was that Father had actually been married before, in Estonia. This truth was finally told to us in 1996. The marriage lasted only a few months, as the wife found herself another man. This is a story Father does not want to tell, but these are the facts in any case. Surely, as I sit here thinking about things now, this may have been another reason why Father left Estonia...

When we speak of things, so long ago, there is also a certain distance to the story telling. Over fifty years have passed.

One day Father gave me a folder with old letters in them. Mother did not know he had done this. I read the letters and realized how important it had been that I could understand Finnish and Estonian, that these languages were open to me. Father's letters were written in

Estonian, but he tried to insert as much Finnish as he could. His first letters are quite funny, because he made completely new and wonderful Finn-Estonian words!

As I read the letters, their content collapsed all time, and I entered the world between two young people very much in love. Letters did not change, were not altered with time. The truth was right before me:

March 2nd, 1944

"Somewhere"

Mirja!

Dearest! Don't be angry with me as I have not telephoned you (translated, the word was used in Finnish, so that it was: have not clobbered you with the phone).

We are not allowed to make personal calls from the phone here. I am sorry to inform you that I have to transfer from my present location to Taavetti, but don't be upset due to this. I will write to you and hope that because of this, our tie will not break...perhaps not even if I might have to go as far as the North Pole – don't you agree?

You are the only one I can write to here in Finland. I hope that our relationship changes, from our small acquaintance to becoming closer friends.

I send to you, with these hopes, my photo, as you requested. I hope for the same from you (a photo). I would be overjoyed if I found one in your letter.

A heartfelt greeting and one sensitive kiss for you!
Alfredo

P.S. Write immediately, I await in loneliness. kpk.2/352

Now Mother goes on with her story: "So Alfred came to my house for vacation, but he didn't have any coffee. My mother was disappointed."

"Yes," Father adds, "I couldn't get the coffee. I gave my money to one boy who was to buy the coffee in Helsinki, but I never got the coffee, nor my money back."

Mother remembers: "We spent the week visiting, though I worked during the day. My job was interesting, in the government. It was with the defence ministry, in Hamina. Remember, at the time, many women did wonderful work; the Lottas helped incredibly in the war effort.

"It was amazing how I got that job. I was taking a secretarial course in Kotka. Every morning I took a bus, and in the bus, I met our neighbour, Jorma. He was a lieutenant in the army, and with him was a captain, who I didn't know. Jorma asked me where I was going. During the bus ride, I was studying. The men had been watching me, and where I was going.

"When I finished the course, Jorma came to my house and asked if I wanted to come and work at the defence ministry. I was surprised. It was quite an honour to be asked, I thought. There was a soldier's circle, or society, and they all loved my handwriting. This was in the winter of 1941. I was working here for a few months before the war started again. I took the recruits as they came in, getting all the paperwork ready, as they signed up for the army. Here I had been working a few years when I met Alfred in February of 1944. By the way," adds Mother triumphantly: "When 'halloo' came on the phone, everyone knew it was 'that' Estonian fellow. His way of greeting over the phone was so different from the Finnish way! He called me."

Father wants to continue. "But now back to when I came to your house. I remember arriving on the train, in Hamina. It was snowing, and there was Maire with those blue eyes. There was something different in those eyes. She smiled at me. At that moment, I took a deep breath, thinking 'this is the girl,' even though her physique was not athletic, her eyes were so blue.

"We arrived at Maire's home in Pitajansaari, a pretty home. Well, it was so special; all the floors were polished. So clean."

Mother adds: "We always had it like this, always."

"Then," continues Alfred, "we had coffee and cakes."

"No, how could we have had coffee when you didn't bring any?" reminds Mother. "Mother made you pancakes."

"Well, I was warmly received, and had sauna too. Maire washed my back."

"Don't lie!" screams Mother now.

"Well, why didn't you come and wash my back?" asks Father.

"Maire's family was the first Finnish family to befriend me. When my vacation was over, I reported back to Taavetti. Hannes Oja remembers the letters I received. Oja stamped the letters 'War Censored. Top Secret.'"

March 24th, 1944

My Maire!

Harmonious thoughts flow in my heart at the moment, a song echoes through this lovely Finnish forest, a forest where I am positioned at the moment – separated from you.

It is a beautiful morning, the sun sparkles and plays on the Spring snow, like crystal, intertwined. There are thousands, thousands of snowflakes!

They are pure, hearts white, they do not hate, are not angry. They don't know how hard this world is, how manipulative and weak people are. No, no, Maire dearest, I want to be good to you, and I want to be everything for you. Our love must be the same: clean and loyal and pure, like snow pearls. The sun cannot go behind the clouds for us or dampen this lovely joy.

I am joyous having you. You make me joyful. If I were to lose you, I would lose my life. Because of my circumstance, I cannot be betrayed another time and I want to have a happy life, happy with you.

Now I close my eyes, almost as in prayer, and you come before my eyes, and I envision our future home. By the beautiful shore of a Finnish lake, a small white house, like a fairy tale. It is surrounded by fields full of flowers. You and I and a little girl, Heljo with blonde curly hair, is holding your hand. We look out into the distance, over the beautiful Finnish forests and lakes, over to that land where I once, when young, fought. From where I was swept across the stormy sea leaving behind my own homeland, which was taken over by strangers' hands. I was a soldier, losing my homeland.

But now I have a homeland and a home, dear Maire and little Heljo. This is what I will one day tell my little one, who will sit by her father's knee and listen to her own father's sad departure and her father's big joy.

Yes, life is beautiful. I believe and hope that these things will one day come true. I have complete trust in you, Maire. Take me, I am yours forever, your Fredi. I give myself to you because you have a good heart. I love you!

I can't explain everything that my heart feels in this letter. We shall talk, talk when we are together: you, me and love! Heartfelt wishes,

Your Fredi

P.S. To your mother, father and Kepa, many greetings.

March 24th, 1944

Maire dear!

I send a second letter of the day to you. I don't know if you have received any of my letters. I have written to you every day and I think that you should have received them. I haven't had even one letter from you. Please do not worry about me as I believe in the seven of hearts.

Write to me all that is in your heart.

Many greetings to all the relatives and for You, I send a hot, hot kiss!

Greetings to you,
Your own Fredy.

P.S. I have sent two letters to Estonia, so that they will send the necessary papers.

Father recollects.

"At Easter Maire came to visit me in Taavetti, and I had sent two boys to meet her at the station, with flowers. I was performing in Kouvola, with the choir, along with the other Estonians. Uno Mankin was here too. He was the key organizer, talented and very personable.

"We put on variety shows. Our regiment, JR200 was a regiment where the Estonian boys were trained in Finnish army tactics, and the language. We had two battalions. The first had come in 1943, and was in the frontier, and now the second one included boys like me. These boys became known as 'Soome Poisid,' or 'Finnish Boys.' Many of my friends, to this day, I met in Taavetti.

"I was helping in the organizing of different cultural events, showing goodwill to the Finnish people. Many boys wanted to perform and join the show, but not everyone had the talent. These shows were very popular. We performed at numerous towns.

"We did not have a dread of fighting anymore. Somehow, with the Finnish army, our logical choice was also a secure choice. But, we did see action, and about two hundred Estonians were killed during this time.

"After our performance in Kouvola, we were scheduled to perform in Helsinki, but had to get back to fight as Russia was again mounting an attack.

"Well, the first of May, 1944, Maire and I were engaged. Of course, I didn't do the asking. Ha, ha. I read about it in the newspaper, in the social notices section. Maire Rautanen was to be married to Alfred Karu. I was so surprised!"

"In reality," says Mother, "after Alfred came back from Taavetti, he came to speak with my parents, asking if they had any objections to him marrying me. My mother laughed, and said, 'Now I understand about the coffee!'"

May 1944

Dear Maire!

One More Time

One more time I would like to see you,
One more time to warmly embrace you,
One more time your beautiful blue eyes
I would like with all my soul to see!

My nicest dream, after all of spring's troubles,
An only kiss I plead from you.
You have penetrated my heart
You have taken over my soul.

Now I linger in this war, protecting the home
so dear which must be for us in the future!

Do you remember the beautiful moment
When with God I left you at the station?
From your blue eyes I saw a tear fall when
we kissed even as the train moved on.

My dearest, think of me at times
And know I live only for You!
One more moment, gift to me
As to others you give thousands!
One more moment's not much to ask
from my intended, my betrothed.
One moment which belongs to me!
in Karjala

I send you these words, written to pass the time. The
song is called "Uks ainus ois ei tohiks olla palju." When
I come on vacation I will sing it to you. Now I end, as I
need to sleep. I send you warm wishes here from this
wilderness.

Your own Fredy

"And so our engagement party was held in Taavetti," Mother
explains. "I had some wine in my suitcase, as well as all kinds of
goodies for the coffee table. The Estonian boys who were invited,
their names are in the guest book we still have. There was nothing in
the stores; we made what we could at home. When you are young,
things seem different. I was optimistic, even though Hamina was
quite close to where the Russians were approaching. There was a lot
of propaganda then, too.

"Russian propaganda. Our future friend, Paavo Airola, was doing
counter-propaganda in Finland, in the Russian language. We were
young and full of hopes."

May 9th, 1944

Maire!

As I promised to write, I indeed shall write. The song on the radio, whirling around, is sad. It speaks of life's truths, and as it happens, it is the way my heart speaks. Now my heart speaks only of you!

As I listen to the music I think of this mixed-up world. A friend (soldier) has been in and out to see me all night, offering me juice and pulla. We spoke for some time, then I told him that I want to write a letter to my own Maire, so I chased him out of my room.

Right now I would like to hug and kiss you a thousand times, passionately. I can't wait through all the days until I can have you beside me, dear Maire.

Dear, I would like to apologize because I can't speak correctly on the telephone. Every time I do, I turn red, and blush when I say words wrong. Truly it is difficult that I can't speak in Finnish. When I come on holiday I ask that you teach me grammatically; it is the only hope I have in learning.

I wish to be a good boy now, as it is already 1:30 a.m. so I will go to sleep. Good night, my nocturnal white dream.

Your own Fredi.

Now Father continues: "On May 21st, 1944, I came to Hamina to get ready for one of our variety shows. It was a big event. Ads all over town. We were a big hit.

Hamina's Newspaper, June 1944:

"Estonian Volunteer Regiment Holds Concert"

Our brother-nation Estonia's volunteer soldiers held a concert last Sunday evening. Though it was raining heavily, the concert hall was full. The energetic and action-packed programme kept the audience attentive right from the start, and as the evening progressed, the warm feelings only increased.

The Estonian musicality was brought out beautifully. The rhythmic and clear voices of the male choir sang a composition by Jurisaari as well as other songs. The soloists – vocal and violin as well as the quartet – received a thunderous applause. Between the songs there were dance performances including folk dances and a lively sailors' dance. A few short Finnish humorous sketches were performed by comedian Netliv, who enthralled the audience with his mimicry of "100" languages as well as hen house noises.

Mr. Grunthal hosted the whole evening briskly and warmly as master of ceremonies. After the unusually long concert, flowers were presented to the visitors.

The Estonian's director, second lieutenant Mankin, gave a few heartfelt words of appreciation. Mayor Maunula brought greetings on behalf of all of Hamina, and after this, three cheers of "Long Live Estonia!" were shouted by the audience. The Estonians responded with three cheers of "Long Live Finland!"

"We did have fun with the concerts, and we hoped to give something extra back to the country that we had now chosen to fight for

"Then, in June there was a major attack, and we left for the front. Maire continued to work for the government. She waved goodbye to us as we left on the train. Somewhere, there is a picture of her, in the middle of some Estonian boys in uniform.

"Eino Kuusela was our colonel. We travelled to Hiitola, then to the front, at Vuokse.

"Everyone was frightened; nowhere is safe. When a young soldier sees his friend, dead with red bloody soil by him, it certainly makes him ask, 'Why? Why do we have to fight?' It has always been the question, throughout history. Always will be. But, little Finland, like little Estonia, wanted to fight for freedom. Two thousand Estonian boys had joined now, and about two hundred died.

"I was in Viipuri when the red Russian flag was raised on Viipuri's tower. It was very sad and painful to watch from the other side of the river.

"Strong, healthy boys did as they were ordered, to ensure that their country would not be lost. We Estonians vowed to fight to the last drop of our blood. We were so opposed to the political tyrant that was Russia.

"The Estonian morale was good, and we were told later by the Finns that we contributed a lot by holding back the enemy during the final attack. So much was lost, so much Finnish land gone. Karelia, Viipuri. But at least Finland was saved as a country, unlike the fate of Estonia.

"The deeds of the Russians were fresh in the minds of all Estonians. Russians had come in 1939, taking in the night at least 20,000 people to Siberia in cattle cars. Children, women, men separated. This is civilization! We were terribly bitter. Before the end of the war, we were given the opportunity in JR200 to go back to Estonia, to fight the Russians there.

"Did we want this? Most of the boys returned – about 2,000 – but I felt I couldn't. This was really wrong tactically. The JR200 boys loaded onto boats, with no weapons. This was in August of 1944. These boys were given over to the Germans as soon as they landed. The Germans then separated and dispersed the Estonians into their own army. Many boys were killed in the front lines. A bad mistake for Estonians. No rifles, no food or water. Like a sacrifice. My friend Paul Toomsalu remembers what happened to him.

"The reason most boys decided to return was to once again see their mothers, their families. With great hopes, they felt they could still save Estonia in some way. Many became prisoners, fled to Germany, or back to Finland or Sweden, as Paul did.

"So I remained in Taavetti with the remainder of our regiment. There were about one hundred Estonians left. One job we had was to search for the Russian paratroopers near Viipuri. These men had come down in parachutes and killed many innocent people – women and children too. This has been noted in history books.

"We saw their tracks, but never did get any. One night, stationed at my post, I heard a soft sound of someone rowing. I flashed a big light in the direction of the sound, but saw nothing. In the morning, we discovered remnants of the boat, but no trace of the men.

"Soon afterwards, I got sick. The cold nights, damp clothes were not good. I got a high fever and was taken to a hospital in Kakisalmi. Here I was for a few weeks. I received letters from my beloved, promising me all kinds of things! Just joking!"

September 1944

Maire!

Do you remember how the ocean's waves circled on the shore's sands? They came from somewhere far away, here to the shores of this new homeland. We stood together watching as the sun set, listening to the music of the waves. We were young and we looked at everything only as passers-by.

Do you remember how I showed you the seagulls on the sea, like a quivering fog they disappeared into the distance? How we laughed, freely, openly, as we walked along the sandy shore, hand in hand.

We were young and in love. And when it grew dark, we made our way through the pine forest towards your home. I remember as we stood by the gates of your house in the dark, and how beautiful our lives felt then. We parted, pressing our hands together like friends shaking each other's hands.

Do you remember dearest, also, how we stood by the shore and sang with the waves – of joy that was not possible, but still, was ours! We watched the seagulls as they disappeared in the sunset. As the darkness came, light and brightness remained for us! Through splendour, I walked you home.

Alfred.

"Of course, my life was also filled with the daily routines and rather boring times spent as a soldier. This life, where I had never wanted to join any army!

"In September I got a vacation. Then an order came to go to Hamina. Yes, I sure had to follow those orders! They were from Maire.

"I arrived a day earlier than was expected, and therefore, walked to Maire's home. When Maire and her mother saw me approaching, the first thing I heard was 'How come you came so early?' But, Maire's mother gave me a warm hug."

Maire now wants to add her version of this tale. "You see, at the end of June, Alfred went to the frontier, and I didn't see him until September, just before we got married. When he came back, all the arrangements had been made. This is why the story of how he was tricked into marrying me has come about!

"Before the marriage, I went to the Parson's office, to apply for permission to marry a foreigner. This had to be cleared by the External Affairs Minister, in Helsinki. Ansten, the parish pastor, first asked me, 'Couldn't you find a Finnish boy to marry? Why an Estonian – and an artist to boot!' But I filled out the forms and the minister signed them. On Alfred's side, the regiment's Pastor Oscar Puhm signed the necessary papers."

With a sparkle in his eye, Father continues his version: "Well, I didn't know anything about getting married. As I've said, the Finnish language was new to me, and I had difficulty with it. I didn't understand. I was with my regiment, and then was ordered to go to Hamina by order of a certain Maire Rautanen! I arrived in Hamina, all was festive and ready. Maire looked at me, and said that my uniform jacket was very poor indeed. So Paavo Teikari lent me his second lieutenant's coat – we took off the stripes and put on the corporal's stars. Maire borrowed her wedding gown.

Wedding: Alfred and Maire, September 10, 1944

"On September 10th, a black car picked me up, an army limousine. Maire was in the car, wearing a white dress. Before I knew it, we were entering Hamina's Lutheran Church. People were crowded outside as well as inside the beautiful old wooden church.

"Earlier, Maire had been repeatedly teaching me to say the words 'I do' ('Tahdon') in Finnish. In my Estonian-Finnish way, I kept saying 'tahton' – with a 't.' So, there I stood, with Maire holding me, pulling me up the aisle, and still coaching me, saying the word 'Tahdon!' We stood before a black-clad minister. Rings were exchanged and then we were walking backwards in quick motion, out of the church! See, this was an old custom!" Father now enjoys his embellishments thoroughly. "Truthfully, we exchanged vows, and of course walked very dignified, out of the church…When we got outside, there was a crowd, waiting. What a happy day – we had a whole life ahead of us, together now!"

"Yes," reminisces Mother. "It was raining in the morning, but the sun shone in the afternoon. The church sure was full of people. Everyone had come to see the Estonian."

"For the reception, we went to the Civil Guard Building where Maire worked. All was ready for the reception. Maire and her mother had baked a lot, and had also given the ingredients, so the local bakery baked a wedding cake. Sugar was hard to come by, and our coffee was a substitute, korviketta, made from grain. Still, everything was festive. The place was filled with people. We sat at a table together, Maire holding tightly to my hand. 'Don't be nervous,' she said. We had a quartet playing. No dancing was allowed, as it was war-time. We had about fifty people at the reception, where Maire's good friend Nina Arhibov played a piano solo.

"Then once again, I was taken by the hand and led into a waiting car. We went to Pitajansaari, to the big home of the Mutraikusti's, who were family friends. The gramophone played and a dance was held. There was no maid of honour, no best man: that wasn't the custom then.

"So our wedding day ended, and we went to Maire's parents' home. There was no honeymoon. There was still a war to fight.

76

"The next day, I had to go back to join the regiment. We were stationed near the front lines, near Kakisalmi.

"On September 19th, 1944, the news came that peace had been declared. The news was heard on radio and then spread like wildfire from one soldier to the next. The quiet, when peace was declared, is what stays in my memory. Many boys wept. So much had been lost. Russia dictated the terms of peace to Finland. These terms would be very hard, and would figure very significantly in many things, certainly in my life.

"There was a sense of bonding with the other boys, who also had come from Estonia. Many of my friends also stayed in Finland, but some chose to continue on to Sweden immediately, while still others had, rather foolishly, gone back to Estonia.

"What did I think then? Well, everything was bittersweet, as I could not forget my own home, my parents and family. I also regretted the loss of so much time. But then I looked forward, happily, to my new life in Finland.

"We packed our belongings and said our farewells. My new friends, who, like me, had risked a lot in this period of time in history, who had lost a lot.

"Boarding the train, I was impatient to get home, home to Pitajansaari, to Maire. All hopes and dreams were ahead of me. When I arrived at the station, there was Maire, holding flowers. Things were now going to be wonderful.

"We lived with Maire's parents for six months – getting a place was difficult right after the war. Soon after, I left for Helsinki, to get my temporary visa – I requested to stay on as a permanent resident, but was denied. So, I had to keep renewing my pass to remain in Finland. This was done in Helsinki, but with the stamp of the Russian Embassy! The government deemed politically, that we Estonians were now Russian. I visited the office of the Foreign Ministry a number of times, as I wanted to live in Helsinki so that I could attend the Art Academy full-time. The man with the power told me, 'Nothing can be promised you. You are living here under a certain risk.' He added: 'I hope you go to Sweden.' I felt very badly about this.

"I also applied for a job as a set designer for the State Theatre in Helsinki, even passed the requirements for this, but again, due to citizenship, was turned down.

"The climate after the war was such that Finland was very much under the Russians' thumb. The Finnish government was loaded with Communists. Also after the war, 'Valpo,' the new Communist guard, was a looming presence. These people wanted to take over Finland – indeed, have a revolution. But luckily they were stopped in time.

"Even though I was Estonian, our life was good. I studied art in Helsinki, whenever I could, with Veikko Vionoja, Onni Oja and other wonderful Finnish artists. Young good painters. This was starvation work, as no one bought paintings after the war. But the spirits were high in the artistic circle. Everyone wanted to develop in a better direction, produce good, honest art work.

"The up-and-coming artists decided to hold an art show in Hamina. But none of us sold anything. Even Vienoja's paintings, priced low, did not sell – today they are worth quite a lot.

"Endel Ruuberg was another Estonian artist in Helsinki during this time. Endel shared a small studio with another artist – there were no beds, only cardboards piled up for makeshift ones. The room was filled with paintings, paints, papers cramming the tiny space. I slept there a number of times, enjoying it. The mice kept us company too, as I recall.

"Continuing painting, I even sold a few. Maire, of course, still kept her job in Hamina.

"We celebrated Christmas in peace. Peace!

"Maire's kind mother had been nursing a bad cold for some time, and she had asthma on top of it. Maire worried constantly, and I kept reassuring her that everything would be fine. But the cough turned to pneumonia. I remember when Maire's mother lay in bed, very sick. She said to Maire, 'Bring me over those paintings that Alfred has done – I would like to look at them. I like them very much; they're good.' The following day, March 29th, 1945, Mrs. Selma Rautanen (maiden name Tanninen) died at the age of 48. A kind and thoughtful woman, who encouraged me. Surely, she must have worried about the future of her daughter, marrying an artist. Her daughter was then five months pregnant with her first child.

"Shortly afterwards, we moved to a small house on Isoympary Street in Hamina. It was a very nice little place. With friends, I put a partition up, to separate the living room from the bedroom. There was a round window in the room, a wooden stove and a small electric burner. Quite the artistic place.

"Hamina is a lovely little town with a lot of history. It was built in 1653 during Swedish rule, sitting beside the Gulf of Finland, making it an important port. The sidewalks in the centre are cobblestone, the layout of the town is circular. The centre, with the Town Hall and church, has streets radiating out, like spokes on a wheel. There is a saying when someone is a little silly or stupid, 'Your head is as dizzy (circular) as Hamina Town.'

"I travelled back and forth to Helsinki, intent on learning as much as possible from the other artists there. Maire and I were also nervously awaiting the arrival of our first-born."

Maire now adds: "On July 22nd, 1945, I took the train to Kotka, to the hospital, as I knew that soon my baby would arrive. No one came with me – it just was not a custom then. It was a Sunday, and that evening at 7:50 p.m., our little Raul was born. He was a healthy wonderful boy! You can understand what it is like to hold your baby in your arms, and to hope and pray that the world will be a kind place for him. We stayed in the hospital almost a week, and then Alfred came and took us home."

Father continues: "The beginning of the new year, in 1946, we opened our own art and picture frame shop in Hamina.

"Enjoying singing, I joined the Hamina Male Choir, which was a great way of increasing my knowledge of the Finnish language. Here, I enjoyed the company of many friends. There was Oke Jokinen, a well-known musician, who would later become the 'voice' on Yleisradio – the State Radio, championing Estonians and their culture, their country. We were also blessed with the friendship of Casi Edelman, who was very talented as a musician. His son, and his grandson, have been well known in music. What's his grandson's name? Anyway, Captain Metsola was also a friend. The men decided to start up a toy factory, making wooden toys. See, there was really nothing to do for these men. Unemployment was very high. Oke did get a job teaching gymnastics at a local school for a period of time. But, after the war, it was very difficult to get jobs. So people tried all kinds of things. There was plenty of space behind our art shop for the factory and this was also ideal for making the picture frames. Our 'Lelu' factory did not flourish as we had hoped – we should have realized that people would not be buying toys, when more necessary things were needed.

"A lovely memory is the table that Aura's dad made for us. It was shaped like an artist's palette. He was very smart, and helped us with technical things in the little toy factory.

"Life at home was good. We watched as little Raul started to crawl, then to walk, then to run. The stages of his development were fascinating.

"Our little family was also growing. Maire, remember that we got our new place just before you were due with the baby?"

"Yes, it was in November 1946. We moved to Pikkuympary (Small Circle) Street. This place had two rooms and a kitchen. We were allowed to rent this place because we were having another child. Yes, I was due to deliver my second child and knew that much packing had to be done for the move to the new place. I kept on packing well into the night, while Alfred and Raul slept. In the early morning, I left a note on the kitchen table: 'I've taken the bus to Kotka.' I left alone, about 6 a.m. When I arrived, I thought that I had come a little too early even. But all went well, and our little Jyri was born, November 25th, in the year 1946.

"While I was in Kotka, Alfred prepared the new place. It was scrubbed thoroughly and was pretty much in order when Jyri and I arrived home. A lovely family – two boys. Raul was just one year and four months older than Jyri.

"Our little home didn't have curtains, so Fredi printed special ones."

"Yes, they were nice!" adds Father.

Mother continues: "I was in a fortunate position in that our dear friends and neighbours owned a store and they got me a bolt of cloth. The store shelves were virtually empty. There really was nothing much in the stores. Finland had enormous war loans to pay off to Russia."

Father goes on: "During this happy time, I also bought a used sailboat from Mimi Ulander. I paid a little for it, fixed it up, as it leaked. I then learned to sail and, before long, took off on painting excursions around Hamina. I just loved sailing, but Maire didn't like it at all. Imagine! She was born on an island (Pitajansaari) and should have learned to swim at least – they were always crossing over on boats. This was before the big bridge was built."

"But," adds Mother, "I never did swim. I was actually a rather sick child, always had ear infections. The water did not interest me at all."

"So, anyway, once, I asked my friend Paavo Pyykkonen to come along to Tammio Island – which is about ten miles from the Hamina Harbour. I had been there to paint, the island inspired me. It's an incredible place.

"Let's sail! Paavo agreed to come. It was a lovely morning; the mist was rising; the sea was quite calm. I love the sea! Gently the wind blew us towards our destination. We were sailing over an hour, and the wind started picking up. By the second hour, the wind was getting pretty fierce and I could see Paavo was turning a little green. I laughed and loved the waves. But after a while, the waves were really quite frightening, very high. A storm had picked up. Poor Paavo! He went inside the little cabin, kneeled, and started praying. One of the side wires broke off, and I called for Paavo to come and help – we have to unfurl the sail a little, the wind was too strong. No help, as the poor man froze in his spot. I kept calm, steadying the boat against the enormous waves. I knew how to balance the boat, take advantage of the wind.

"We rose and fell, heaving with a height of about a three-storey house. It didn't seem that we were getting anywhere. I started to wonder – where is Tammio? Were we going in the right direction? I couldn't admit it, but I had no idea where we were! The wind was blowing a certain way and should steer us to the right location, I thought, and hoped, with my crude navigational skills. My instincts were guiding me. Oh, no, I had no compass!

"Sure enough, luck was with us – I spotted the island! The wind was too strong to come in on the usual side, so I steered to the leeward side of the island, where I found a gentler cove. We finally clambered to shore, and Paavo, trembling, screamed at me, 'I'll never ever, ever come on your boat again! You're crazy!' And he didn't sail with me anymore, though we were still friends.

"People had been gathering around the shore, watching us as we bobbed on the sea – these people were alarmed, as they had witnessed drownings, so they stood and held their breath until we were safely on shore. You know, we had no lifejackets, no compass. Oh, boy, crazy was right. But of course, when you have a great sailor, that's the most important thing! Ha!

"At Tammio Island, we stayed on the second floor of a lovely wooden house, painted a pale yellow. This was the Suomalainen's place. It was a spotless home, with hand-woven rugs, shining wooden floors. I remember eating the best fish soup of my life here.

"Paavo and I spent a few weeks painting on this island. The shapes and colours of the smooth rocks, the quaint houses and little paths inspired me. From morning till night, we painted, each in our own areas, in silence, as it should be. I got to know the Suomalainens, feeling a special bond with them. At night, we talked a lot together about all kinds of things.

One day, I mentioned to Mr. Suomalainen that I sure would love to live on this island – I'd build a little cabin and paint Tammio life. A few days later, the gentle Finn came up to me, while I was painting. In his heavy accent he said, 'Listen, come with me for a walk.' I followed, and we walked to the shore. The man stopped, and pointed to a large rock. 'From this rock to that tree over there, and then over there to that curve in the land: understand? I want to give this piece of land to you.'

"I was amazed. What a wonderful thing to do. 'But this is a very big gift, how could I accept this?'

"He replied, 'You have fought for Finland's freedom and you are a nice Estonian boy. I want to give this to you.' I was very touched by this man's good heart. Nothing came of this as my fate was destined elsewhere – but hey! I've got a piece of property on Tammio. Of course, this was never written down."

Father chuckles now, as I remember how, forty-five years later, fate would lead us back to this special place. My family had come on a visit along with my parents. Kind relatives owned a big boat, and had treated us to a day of boating – taking us to Tammio Island. There, as we travelled, I watched as my parents held each other, Father teasing Mother. They were remembering their youth. My own children were napping in the cabin of this big boat: how were they to know that we were travelling to a special place, and that old footsteps could still be heard? We finally reached the big dock of Tammio Island. I was fascinated by the smooth lovely rocks, the picturesque, historic island. It was really an idyllic place. As we moored, an old man approached the boat. "Hi there! Where are you folks from?" Our relatives explained that they were showing us the island – we were from Canada, and one of the guests was an artist. The old man then said something quite astonishing: "Well, I remember, after the war, an Estonian artist used to come with his sailboat, and paint here." I had been listening, while my parents were in the cabin, getting their coats and camera.

I yelled, "Well – that Estonian artist – he's here! He's here!"

The man opened his mouth: "Really? Well, well, this is incredible! Come ashore! Come ashore! I'll show you all around the island!"

So, we had a first-rate tour of this place, tracing the paths where Father spent such happy times. The man even opened the museum for us, and as it turned out, he was a cousin of Mr. Suomalainen of so many years ago. I could have stayed on that island – there is a certain wonderful feeling in a place that has not been ruined by so-called progress, where historic details are treasured. There is a sense of quiet stillness, a peace, on an island like this, even though all around it lies an incredible ocean. Yes, Father sure knew a good place when he saw it. That day, I felt sad too, as I saw that now Father was no longer young. I followed behind the entourage, watching my parents' feet, their footsteps, along the old winding paths. A special day in our lives. We took many pictures of the island, and later, I wove a tapestry of the museum window, in memory of all that had been, all that now was: a window looking in and out. A window where the reflection has much meaning.

We sailed back to Hamina late that evening; the sun was setting as we slid into the harbour. My parents' faces flashed before my eyes just as the sun was gone: they were happy and perhaps bewildered. They were survivors.

Now, let's turn back to 1946.

Father remembers: "We didn't sail back that time. We took the ferry boat, and later, my sail boat was brought back behind a motor boat. I painted a lot, and a few good paintings were born. These were strong paintings, strong colours. I took some of them to the Art Academy's professor, Unto Kaipanen. He had just come back from Paris at the time. I showed him my paintings, and asked, 'Tell me, what is wrong; what can be corrected in these paintings?' Kaipanen stood a long time and looked at the work.

"'Well, the only problem I see is that you should use a larger brush. You have a good sense of colour. Just keep going, building your colours, achieving a quiet surface with a broader brush.'

"Kaipanen was a highly-regarded artist, teacher and critic. His own work was very good, and he did use a very smooth touch applying the paint to the canvas. I respected many Finnish artists of this time.

"In October of 1947, there was a juried art show in Helsinki and I took some paintings in. Luckily I was accepted for this show. Today, one of the paintings is at the Taavitsainen cottage! We had a nice life, Maire, the children, and I. Our little business, my art, lots of music and culture.

"During this juried show, my life, our lives, would fall apart.

"It was October 1947. Raul was two years, three months old, Jyri was eleven months old. Maire was due with another baby in January. She was six months pregnant. A lot to do, keeping the children happy, keeping things running. We had great evenings together with friends. We always had company and poor Maire would try to make food from almost nothing. A friend would jokingly come in and say, 'Maire, make some real coffee, not that dribbled water!' We had no real coffee still. The Lehmosvaaras, who owned the bookstore in Hamina, the Edelmans, Jokinens, and the Malinens were frequent guests. Henry Malinen had his own photo studio, and had studied art at the Athenium, the Art Academy in Helsinki."

Mother recounts: "I made a lot of lamb with dill; we really never went hungry. The days and months went by. We were young; the whole world was ours. We barely thought of the fact that Alfred was Estonian. His Finnish was improving rapidly and I was learning Estonian, something that I really enjoyed."

Irritated, Father says, "Alright, Maire, now let's continue. I was talking about the art show in Helsinki. We had plans to continue this show in Hamina, so I had come again, with Hami Lehmosvaara, to make plans. Hami left after a day, but I remained, staying at Linda Nieminen's place – you remember, she was a great supporter of artists. There, I met Sven Ise, who was living at Linda's house. He was an Estonian like me, but his father held a post as a diplomat with the government – he was in England...Sven was studying to be an engineer at the University of Helsinki. We went about our tasks, meeting in the evenings. It was wonderful keeping up with the lives of other Estonians, and also making new friends in Helsinki and Hamina.

"As usual, I had to call on those two dear aunts of Maire's, Engla and Edla. Neither had ever married, and were certainly not at all like Maire – they were quite big. But they were very nice and fed me well! They plied me with food, constantly!

"Returning to Linda's house later that day, I whistled as I walked up to my room on the second floor – but noticed that all the doors were ajar. I walked up quickly, saw papers and things strewn about, two men standing in my room. I said, 'What business do you have here?' I thought they were burglars.

"'We are Valpo police. Who are you? Do you have papers showing your identification?' I froze. I had no papers then, as they were in the process of being renewed at the Ministry office. I had a sinking feeling in my chest.

"Entering the room, I noticed that all my things had been searched through as well. I just didn't understand, didn't know what to think.

"'Can you accompany us to headquarters? We need you to come and verify that we have confiscated Ise's papers.' The Valpo police, as you know, were the Finnish Communist police, different from the regular Finnish 'white' policemen. This did not bode well at all. Sven was accused of espionage! Because his father was in England, as a diplomat, the twisted accusation was made. This was a bad shock for me. What were these people up to?

"I was stuck. No alternative. I was taken to headquarters on Ratakatu. I was shoved through the door. Coldly. Right into a cell. I was in Valpo's jail. There I sat, the whole world was spinning. This was unbelievable. I asked the guard why I was in jail. No answer. The sounds and echoes of strangers, who now controlled me. Locked. After some time, I was questioned. The 'hearings' began.

"These people knew everything about me: that I had been an officer in the Russian army, gone to officers' school, how I had escaped. Under paragraph 58, of the new law, I was a traitor, a Russian traitor.

"My reasons for capture were political. It would be justified, they added, that I be shot. 'So, now sign your name here, Karu!'

"'Why? What am I signing? I have nothing to say and will not sign. There are big spaces between each line – you can fill these blanks with anything you wish, after my signature. No way.'

"I was roughly taken back to my cell, and the door slammed shut. What now? What was Maire going to do? How could I get in touch with her? This was truly ridiculous!"

I see that Mother is now very agitated, she didn't want Father to speak about this time, not today. Another time, not now, she says. I gently press them on and then Mother directs her thoughts back to that time:

"It was a Friday that Fredy was taken. He was to come home that night, the 17th of October. I had gone with the boys to the train station to meet him, but to my surprise, he didn't arrive. We returned home, and I was not particularly concerned, as often he would stay longer than he had planned originally. The next day, we again went to the station. I was getting annoyed, angry. Where was he?

"On Sunday, it was my 24th birthday. Surely he would not miss this! I started to panic when still there was no sign of Alfred. This was really not right. But where did I get in touch with him? I really had not been paying attention to where he was going to stay. Also, in those times, we rarely used the phone. I was in truth also angry at Alfred for not coming home when he was supposed to. I was hurt. He could have phoned me! But my hurt feelings turned to worry and panic when still, on Monday, there was no news. He would get a piece of my mind when he got back! He even missed my special day!

"Tuesday morning, Mirjam Lehmosvaara, who lived just across the street, banged on my door. I let her in. She had a very worried, anxious look on her face. 'Maire, have you read today's paper yet?' I hadn't had the time to do so. I grabbed the paper from Mirjam; she pointed to the article and I read: 'Our town's resident, Estonian artist Alfred Karu, has been detained in Helsinki on Valpo matters, awaiting deportation to Russia.' I almost fainted.

"Impossible! I was then living on nothing but nervous energy.

"Immediately I set to work on how to get Alfred out of this. There had to be a way! Soon, Linda Nieminen called from Helsinki, giving me the news that I had just read. She too had been in the dark as to where Alfred had gone.

"I arranged for sister Kerttu to babysit the boys, and in two days, I was in Helsinki. I was now furious. I had no fear. I arrived at the Valpo jail, there on Ratakatu. Even though I was six months pregnant, nothing stopped me. I demanded to know what was going on. I demanded to see my husband. 'Yes, yes, madam, we see that this whole thing has affected your husband badly.'

"'Of course it hurts when he is innocent, and there is no reason for him to be held!' I stormed. 'Let him out! What are your reasons?'

"Nothing helped. Alfred was trapped in his cell. What had he done wrong? He had come to help Finland after all was lost in Estonia. Now this unjust and terrible tactic of those in control in Finland would strike a hard blow. Nameless faces had concocted this special paragraph that would destroy so many lives. But what else is new? These things have happened during all of history, and are still happening. But why the Finnish government allowed this is still something that bothers me a lot.

"We felt betrayed by Finland. My own country, full of Communists, I thought. These people were taking charge, while the Finnish government turned its back to this issue.

"Alfred was allowed out. We sat at a table, and were allowed to speak for a few minutes. When the accused came out, he looked pale and weak. 'Maire, Maire – now what must we do? How are you? I am so sorry…' I hugged my husband, but the feeling I had was like someone had died. I promised to do whatever I could to free him from this incredible predicament. 'Don't worry, keep calm!' I said bravely.

"I left to go back to Hamina, the shop had to be taken care of, the children, our lives, our lives. Panic and bewilderment. My father, sister and friends were there to support me. How I made it through the days is astounding. I felt like a robot. The boys were so innocent, had no idea what adults were doing in this world. Their lives seemed secure.

"As soon as possible, I hurried back to Helsinki, met with Linda Nieminen and, through her, got acquainted with other Estonians. I also got a good Finnish lawyer, Nykanen. We went to the State Council, to the Foreign Ministry, everywhere, to turn any stones that would help. I spoke to Urho Kekkonen, the Foreign Minister. He was to become the President of Finland later. We tried every avenue. Another Finnish woman, Kaija Sirell, was also very active with me. When we went to the Council, we were told that if the command to imprison Karu would have come from Russia, as they were saying at Valpo headquarters, then it would have cleared through the Council. It had not crossed their desks, so it was obviously the handiwork of Finland's own Communists. I know now that many Communists were hoping for high honours and praise if they could do something to show how keenly Communist they were – and this act of sending the Estonians back – back to Russia – was one such act.

"I started to make noise. We went to the newspaper, and this tale was printed. Due to my small efforts, at least the timing for deportation was being stalled. I was told by someone at the Council that these men would already have been sent off to Siberia (as many before them were) had it not been for the press coverage and the rising awareness now that such things were taking place. This was hidden – people didn't know about this.

"Truly, I was active. Like you, Marjut. I wouldn't give in, I was a fighter then.

"The reporters were interested in our story, and the papers were full of the news."

Helsinki, November 1947 *Helsingin Sanomat*

Member of Parliament, Arvo Salminen has put the following questions to Cabinet: Does the government know that the State Police have now, for a number of years, detained Estonians who have legally resided in this country for many years, and whose actions have not been in any way illegal or harmful to the country? What measures are the government going to take in order to investigate this matter thoroughly and to punish those officials who have possibly committed illegal actions?

Another article in the Helskinki *Sanomat*

"Uncertain Undertakings"
Valpo's instigated holding of Estonians has raised concerns here as well as outside our borders. We here in Finland have become accustomed to a lot that would never have been possible during normal times. We also understand that the holding of the Estonians could well hinge on the authority of the peace agreement's article.

However, the public has not been assured that this is the case. There is distrust and concern that the whole undertaking is that of Valpo and its protector, the minister of the interior, Mr. Leino's own doing. This has been strengthened these past few days, as it appears that indeed the Minister of the Interior can effectively appeal to Russian quarters regarding these commands. But these commands have come after Valpo was more than willing to complete its detainment of the Estonians. This also points to the fact that Valpo is still continuing its witch hunt.

The Social Democrats have always taken the view of protecting human rights...without the Democrats, during the last war, the Finnish Jews would have been forced to Nazi death camps. We have for these reasons moral obligations to demand from this government if they have a "new face" and to uncover and truthfully explain the reasons behind giving these refugees up to a foreign country. (submitted by the Social Democrat Party, Helsinki.)

"Alfred was moved after a few weeks' time to Katajanokka Prison," continues Mother. "What a feeling – my husband was not a criminal! He was a pawn in the games of politics.

"The weather was turning cold; the winds seemed to blow right through me, as I walked to the prison to see my husband. But only once did I have to stand in the line up outside, waiting, waiting with others who came to see their loved ones. I thought, no, I can't stand in this line, waiting. It was cold. The prison guards were very nice and I talked with one of them, who suggested I call the prison official to request permission to come whenever I wanted. So I did this and was granted my request. I was also allowed to take Alfred paints, brushes, some paper. Here, imprisoned, were top military men, Finland's own generals and ministers. What a time in Finland's history!

"I start to get dizzy when I remember this," adds Mother.

Father goes on: "It is hard to explain unless you live it yourself. I didn't do anything wrong, had committed no crime. Yet here I was, in a cell, four feet by eight feet, behind a lock. Then you read on the walls 'Long live freedom! See you in Siberia!' scribbled by a previous prisoner. What was the reason I was here? I had joined the Finnish Army to help – and here I was. The Finnish government had to give back all foreigners to Russia and they sure knew who those foreigners were!

"Yes, and then you sit there in the darkness. The cot was only pulled down from the wall at night. During the day I sat on a stool. My mind was working overtime with the thoughts that my life was finished. My family, my art, all my hopes were gone. Looking back at my life, I saw how many times I had been knocked down with trouble, had been forced to be in armies I never wanted, had lost so much…At the age of twenty-eight, here I was. Anger and fear turned to complete despair. I sat day in and day out, holding my head in my hands.

"Then something incredible happened. I saw a streak of light –

really. It was as if it came from Heaven's skies down to me. I heard a voice, and the voice said, 'Don't worry, as your son will save you.' A wonderful feeling of peace came over me, and my heart was no longer heavy. I wondered if I had seen a vision – whatever it was, I knew that this was real. Very real. But what did this mean? My heart was not heavy, and I felt that someone would guide us. This 'vision' truly was a very powerful event in my life.

"As Maire said, I was taken to Katajanokka Prison. It's an old stone prison, built during the Czar's time. Huge steps, stone floors, little light. Once inside, we were told to take our civilian clothes off and were given prison clothes. Stripes, baggy, all the same. My new uniform. A new uniform once again forced on me. I was now a criminal. I can't remember my number.

"Then I was pushed into a cell where, before me, must have been a crazy person, or a person turned crazy. The mattress was torn to pieces, the stool was broken, a real mess. I was escorted to another cell.

"Then the progression of other Estonians began. In came Paul Saar, many 'Soome Poisid' or 'Finnish Boys' who had voluntarily joined the Finnish army. Paul was put in my cell. He had been captured the same day as I, on the 16th of September. He too had married a Finnish woman, had a son, our Raul's age. His son's name was Pekka. My cell mate was continuing his studies for the Lutheran ministry in Helsinki at the time. This man felt his religious ideals deeply, yet was never pushy, only kind and sympathetic to all the inmates. Paul's life would dramatically lead to another place.

"The prison was full. At this time, the Russians blamed Finnish generals and military men. Mannerheim's right hand man was here too. Even Finland's President was taken. You see, the government was really weak and full of Communists wanting to please Mother Russia.

"The morning food line was repulsive. There was a huge pot, in which the soup was made. Through an open door, I saw as the same pot was also used as a latrine. I saw this, as the pot was dumped and washed. At least it was washed.

"Maire brought me my paints, and I was allowed to spend some time sitting in the middle of the corridor, sketching. I saw the high windows, and bright light outside. Deep shadows and darkness fell on us below. I still have a few of these watercolours. I also painted one of Paul Saar sitting beside two other prisoners, and one of the Salvation Army singers, who came there to try to cheer us up.

"There was a con artist in jail too. He had lied and endeared himself to many women, then taken off with their money. He had disguised himself as a ship's captain, a flyer, a baron. He had all kinds of aliases, but the common line was that he had a 'temporary' problem with his funds. Would the dear lady please see it in her heart to lend him some money just until his accounts were settled? This man was small, but he sure had a big mouth! But now he sat in jail, and sang religious songs. He even sang the evening grace. It was actually humorous in a way, for me, because of my own situation. His problems seemed small. He kept us all amused.

"Paul was a wonderful person. He was continually studying theology, religion, but he never tried to push his views on anyone. In any case, Paul gave us strength.

"The days dragged on. I drew many faces in prison. We had sixteen Estonians in my area at the time. Many from Inkeri were also imprisoned. I heard that Sven Ise was also here, though his cell was not near mine. What had happened to him, when did the Valpo get him, I wondered.

"Every morning we were given a ten-minute walk time outside, so on one of these 'outings' I switched my number with Sven's cell mate. This way, I got in to see Sven, and we started to plan how we could escape from this place – what the possibilities were. I had all kinds of fantastic ideas. The only way would be when we could be taken out to questionings.

"Actually, Sven did manage to escape, for a short time. He was taken out by taxi, to be questioned at Valpo headquarters. Sadly, Sven was sent to Siberia, serving the 25 years plus five years.

"Meanwhile, Maire was doing her best, with other Estonians and Finns, to seek release of the men."

Helsinki newspaper, November 1947

"More Explanations Needed Regarding Estonians Being Held. Petitions for Two Arrested, to Go to Parliamentary Commission Tomorrow, Say Arrested Men's Wives."

The imprisoned Estonians (Valpo states there are thirteen), continue to await the decision. Tomorrow it will be three weeks since the first arrest. At the moment, eleven are held in the Provincial Prison, and two are under Valpo's protection. A petition to the External Affairs Minister has been presented, regarding Alvre, Sirell, Karu and Saar. Tomorrow, a lawyer representing Sirell and Karu makes his appeal on their behalf to the Parliamentary Commission. The Minister's office has the requests and other papers concerning them, as well as Valpo's minutes of the hearings on hand for consideration. It appears that the matter will go before the Security Council before long. This will be heard by both Foreign Ministers, which Prime Minister Pekkala will be presented with. It appears that he will not have time to look into this matter before his trip to Moscow.

It may be mentioned that the prisoners have been informed recently that they could renew their residency permits, which are already valid, by another year. These permits are renewable a year at a time.

"Arrested Men's Wives Give Their Account"

Two charming, yet, serious young women, from whose eyes sometimes could be seen a downcast smile, sat across from us yesterday evening as we visited the home of one of the young Finnish-Estonian families, whose provider has sat for three weeks in the Provincial

Prison. The women are engineer Vaino Sirell's wife and Mrs. Maire Karu, artist Alfred Karu's spouse.

During the half hour interview this reporter caught glimpses of two very happy young Finnish-Estonian marriages up until now.

Vaino Sirell escaped to Finland in the Fall of 1943, fleeing days before he would have been forced into the German army. The burn marks on his hands told of a half a year of hard trials in the German prison camps. In Finland, he joined the army alongside his fellow countrymen (other Estonians). He was not at the front, but was stationed in Turku and Helsinki on maintenance duties. When peace was declared he got a job as an engineer in the technical department of the National Radio.

"And then we met and got married in 1945," said Mrs. Sirell. "Our little Tom will be three months tomorrow. We waited in earnest for our baby, and now my husband misses his son greatly, while sitting in jail. Every time I visit, I must tell my husband how our son is doing, how much he has grown. It wasn't easy to leave his (my husband's) homeland, home and family, but this had to be lived through."

Finland began to feel like home to Vaino Sirell, as it does to so many who we share a kinship with, who come from other countries. He founded a home here and this is where he decided to settle, as he saw no reason why he should not be able to. He didn't think that he had broken any laws against Finland or our big neighbour, and so the Sirells lived peacefully and with youthful optimism in a one-room flat, with a temperamental hot plate, like so many other young couples. Until one evening three weeks ago, when Mrs. Sirell was home alone and three Valpo men stepped in unexpectedly. Engineer Sirell was out at the time and when he arrived home he was arrested. "I thought he'd return the same evening," stated Mrs. Sirell, "but he still hasn't come. The worst is that I don't know when he will be freed and what he has been charged with. We are trying to wait patiently and he is certainly worth waiting for. He is the best human being I know. I wouldn't change him for anything!"

Alfred Karu arrived in Finland the same time, November 1943. He had tried to put off going into the German army by giving a poor health report, but when this failed and there was no other recourse, Karu defected to Finland. He served here in the army with the same regiment. After the war, Karu, who enjoys painting, settled in Hamina where he also has a framing business. His young wife Maire is from Hamina and so this young couple understandably feels completely at home in that little town. "My husband is a very happy active person. He has many friends," notes Mrs. Karu. The young Estonian is one of the most enthusiastic members of the Hamina Male Choir, the Arts Club and Sailing Club. The Karus have two children, both boys. The oldest is two and the youngest is eleven months in age and a third child is expected. Karu was arrested three weeks ago when he was in Helsinki on a visit. "I have been in Helsinki these weeks so I could visit my husband in jail. Our shop is closed and is operating at a loss. My sister is caring for the children there at home and explains to our two-year-old that 'Father will come soon' when he asks where Father is. We try to hope that everything will work out and that things will still be settled so that we will again have a father who will care for us, as sweetly as he has up to now."

The families of the prisoners have been allowed to visit every day, and the women said that the guards and other prison authorities have been friendly and understanding. The wives were happy a few days ago when they went and saw that their husbands had been allowed, once again, to dress in civilian clothes. "It was truly awful when at first we saw them in prison clothes as though they were criminals, even though they don't know who they have offended."

Now Mother continues: "I travelled back and forth to Hamina, making sure that the boys were well, and to see if anything could be done for the business. Luckily family and friends were willing to help. At night it was very difficult, and I wrote letters to Alfred, letters that did not tell him of everything, of my newest concern:

November 10th, 1947

Fredy dear,

Many loving greetings to you from Hamina! I came home last night, as we discussed on Saturday.

The children and Kerttu were sleeping at 10:10 p.m. when I arrived. As I had no key, I kept knocking on the door, but Kerttu did not wake up. So I went over to Mirjam and Ami's and Ami went over a few times, knocking on the window but we could not get in, so I stayed overnight at their place.

In the morning when I woke up, I immediately went to the window, to see if anyone was moving about in our house, and I saw little Raul's blond head at the window.

This day has passed; it is 10:30 p.m. as I write this. Jyri is sleeping already, in his favourite position, but Raul is still up. The boys are well and are waiting for their beloved father to return home – they both clasped their little hands together as we said the evening prayer, so that God will send our dear father home. So, dearest, you know the great love and longing with which we think of you and hope for the day when we once again have you with us.

I have an incredible loneliness for you, that I cannot even express in words. The whole house feels so empty without you, dear. When I was in Helsinki and had permission to come to see you I felt so much better.

Dear Fredi, we must believe and trust in the Lord, as He is the only one who can help. When we believe in Him with all our hearts, and trust in Him, and ask for His help, then with His power everything will turn out well.

Here it has been snowing tonight so that the earth is all white, but the weather is quite warm, not as chilly as in Helsinki. My cough is almost gone.

Kerttu is going to the shop tomorrow. We will keep it open for now, at least for a few days, so that we can get those finished works out, etc.

When I will come to visit you, I am not certain of yet. Unless something untoward happens, it should be Sunday, though I will be in touch with how things are going there the whole time.

Dearest, now I'll go to bed, as Rauli began crying and he won't sleep it seems, until I, too, go to bed.

Dear, let's believe that, with God's help, everything will turn out well. Wishing you everything that is good, loving wishes and a good night's kiss.

Your Maire, Raul and Jyri.

"One day," says Father, "Maire came to see me, handed me a sandwich. I saw that she was very disturbed. She looked awful, had a sorrowful face. I was very alarmed. "Rauli is sick. I've brought him to the Children's Hospital" (in Helsinki).

Silence now, even now, in my living room, as Father talks of this time. Mother takes a deep breath and continues:

"I travelled back and forth from Hamina to Helsinki. Kerttu looked after the boys. I closed our business temporarily and spent all my time trying to get Alfred free. I arrived back in Hamina very late one night and, as all was dark at the house, decided to go and talk things over with the Lehmosvaaras across the street. I fell asleep at their house and, early in the morning, walked over to our home.

"As I walked up, there was little Raul, with his blond hair, looking at me through the window. What I didn't say in the letter to Fredy was my worry about Raul...

"I looked at my little boy. I was alarmed. My heart stopped. His look, something in his eyes was not right. He was sick. We have a photo taken of Raul at this time...I took him to the doctor after a few days, but the doctor rudely told me 'There is nothing wrong with the boy – the problem is you. You are too nervous. The child needs nothing more than malt juice.'

"I replied, 'Listen, Doctor, surely you have heard of our situation, and if I'm nervous about this, I cannot help what has happened in my family. But I think that my son is sick. Something is not right.'

"I was upset, frightened. The doctor stood his ground, and I left. I felt in my heart that something more had to be done, to ensure that yes, yes, Rauli was alright.

"There was a town nurse who I knew, so I walked over to her place. Knocking on the door, holding on to Raul, I hoped that my instincts were wrong, that it was all in my head. The woman answered, and I blurted out: 'Rauli is sick. Can you please help? Can you get me an appointment to see Professor (Arvo) Ylpo at the Helsinki Children's Clinic?' The kind nurse immediately called, and so, within a few days we went to see the specialist. Rauli was not himself: he hardly slept; he had a fever; and his eyes looked blurred. The poor little child could not really tell me what was wrong: how did a child a little over two years tell anyone how he felt?

"Professor Ylpo was a very friendly doctor. I believe he was one of the top children's doctors in Europe. A small man with large hands. After looking at Raul, checking him, he turned towards me and said, 'I am sorry, Mrs. Karu, but Raul must remain in the hospital. He has spinal meningitis.'

The world collapsed. I almost stopped breathing. 'No, no, no.' And that doctor in Hamina, telling me that nothing was wrong! Could things have been better with faster action? We wasted time. I don't know. Maybe it would have helped if things could have been caught earlier – who knows?"

November 27th, 1947

Fredy dear!

I write this to you in case I don't get to see you because of that vihamieslakon moksi! (strike) Dearest, how have you slept the night, and otherwise, how are you feeling?

I slept well and Raul slept well. I just called the nurse – Raul's temperature is 39.2 degrees but he slept the whole night peacefully. Dear little Raul! Whatever happens, it is God's will, and that is best.

Dear, stay calm and try to endure this, as God does not give more of a burden than one can bear. Let's believe that everything turns out well, with God's help!

Wishing you strength and peace.

Loving wishes,
Your Maire

Now, in 1997, I sit and cry for my brother, that brother who I have always missed. Was it because of you, Rauli, that I always felt that someone was missing at the table, missing at family get-togethers? I would often count, just to be sure that we had the family together; the feeling was very strong. I cry for a brother who I would have loved to have known, who might have been a million things.

I can now understand those silent times when Mother would just sit in the corner of the living room, not talking. Sorrow in her eyes. I feel my mother's tears, my father's tears.

Father is pacing rapidly now; he is walking back and forth. My parents are unveiling hidden facts, and I want to know, I always wanted to know!

The story continues, Mother getting her voice back: "Raul was in the Children's Hospital, and I stayed at Aunt Edla and Aunt Engla's apartment. I can't remember how many days this was. How many days was Raul in hospital? A week or so…maybe less. During this time, there was no medicine for Raul, so a special delivery came from Sweden by airplane. This was a medication that was injected into his legs. Raul was getting worse. The medication did nothing. Then Raul slipped into a coma. I hoped and hoped and prayed. Please save my little son.

"I got a letter from Dr. Ylpo, stating what condition Raul was in, and I hurried to take this to Katajanokka Prison authorities. I requested permission for Alfred to come and visit his dying son. This was November 26th.

"Jyri was in Hamina, and had celebrated his first birthday without his parents, the day before. Thankfully Kerttu and my father were taking care of things in Hamina.

"Well, the permission was granted for visitation. Alfred was given his civilian clothes to wear, and arrived at the hospital with two guards, the Valpo Communist guards. They entered Raul's isolated room. There lay Rauli, enclosed in a kind of tent-like structure. The two guards stood with feet apart, pistols at their sides. One glanced at his watch and said, 'Ten minutes' time,' and began timing.

"I went wild. I shouted, 'Don't you have any heart at all? Look, this child is dying. The father will see his son for the last time!'

'Well, five minutes more then,' was the sharp and cold reply. I asked if more could be given, but now I don't remember if more was granted, but it was a horrible shock. I could do nothing but cry. Words cannot express the situation."

Mother goes on: "I was at Raul's bedside, the little boy so weak. Alfred and I sat by Rauli's side, stroking him, praying silently. Our boy was slipping away. Our time was up. Alfred was taken away. I stayed late that night, and then went to my aunts' apartment to sleep. Raul died early the following morning, on November 27th..."

Everyone is quiet now. We do not move. I do not want to cry now, not now. I gently ask Mother, "What did you do?"

"I went to the prison to tell Alfred. Told him I was going to Hamina to arrange for the funeral and everything. Also I had to get an application form from the parson in Hamina in order that Alfred might be allowed to come to the funeral. My aunts arranged for the coffin and then my father drove with a taxi from Hamina to come and get Rauli and me. Rauli in his coffin.

December 4th, 1947

Fredy dearest!

Loving greetings to you as I write here, on the kitchen table. Jyri is fussing a little; he just woke up and wanted some milk. He is doing well, only he has become quite the lap-baby. Father has spoiled him too much during the time I was in Helsinki.

As you know, Father came to get us on Sunday. He had hoped to come to see you, but was unable to as we left at 1 p.m. We took little beloved Raul to Pitajansaari.

You can imagine and understand how desolate and dismal it was to come home, now with Raul away – I didn't see him or hear his voice. The little white bed stands empty in the corner, waiting for him. Now Raul feels fine; he has no more pain or sickness; he has no more distress – he is happy.

> I'm a plant in the garden of Heaven
> In the care of a knowing gardener.
> He guides the clouds and the weather
> And tends to all of His flowers.
> I'm a lamb of the dear shepherd
> – am the smallest of the herd to Jesus.
> The cruel world can't swallow you
> When Jesus looks on by the road.
> (translated loosely)

These are the words to that lovely spiritual (written by Hilja Haahti).

Little Raul was too fragile for this life and God saw better than we. He gathered Raul to Him, to the place where the storms of this world do not reach. Little Raul, from on high, looks at us – he sees his father there in prison, innocent, with heavy heart, grieving. He sees his mother and little Jyri here at home.

Little Jyri, as though he understands all of this, has been like a ray of sunshine during this sadness. He has incredibly changed in looks, to Raul's looks. I don't know if I imagine this, but this is how it appears to me.

I phoned the lawyer. He will arrange your release for the funeral.

Dear Fredy, let's hope that you will be allowed to come, so that we can send Rauli to his final resting place, together. Let's pray to the Lord so that you will be able to come, and also that everything will be cleared up by that time, so that you can all return home from prison.

Dearest love, now I end this, as I feel very tired. If you feel up to it, please write. I am so lonely as I have not heard anything from you.

Your Maire and Jyri.

"So then I knocked once again, on the parson's door. Ansten was the one who had asked me why I had to choose an Estonian to marry. He was very helpful now, and together, we arranged things. It took two weeks before clearance was given for Alfred to come. We buried Raul on December 14th.

Everything was arranged in Hamina. I didn't go to Helsinki anymore. I was also now eight months' pregnant. We printed the death notices as was the custom then."

Mother's thoughts now are scrambled; it is painful to remember. She speaks in fragments: "This was at the graveyard. Some members of the Hamina Choir came and sang by the grave. How this was all arranged...

"Alfred arrived in Hamina the night before the funeral, and well – well, don't write this down, many people have gone through this type of thing, even worse," adds Mother now.

Still, Mother does continue:

"Our friend, a policeman, came over to tell me that Alfred had arrived at the police station. 'Can we go and see him?' I asked. Well, whatever, I did go and see him, and Alfred was allowed to come home for the night. A Communist policeman was ordered to escort Fredy, in handcuffs, from Helsinki, but this guard became ill, and was replaced by an ordinary policeman, not Communist. This person was ordered to come from Turku to Helsinki for the job. Alfred and the policeman came then to our home for the night. Then some of our friends arrived, and they made a point of speaking to Alfred. The policeman was very kind and sympathetic. He left us, to go out for a walk. 'I feel so badly that this kind of thing can happen,' he said.

"One of our friends asked the guard, 'What would happen to you if this Karu suddenly escaped?'

"'Well, nothing more than I would be fired,' replied the kind policeman.'"

I look over at Father now. He is very agitated. Almost as though he is still worried someone will get him, take him away. "Let's not talk about this time; I can't do it. Let's talk another time, not today."

Again, I ask softly: "Father, I would like to know what was happening from your perspective...tell me about that time..."

"I had heard the news from Maire that Rauli was sick. I can't tell anyone how hard this was. I was useless to anyone. I was escorted to the hospital to see my son. The pistols were in the hands of the guards. We drove to the hospital, walked up to the second floor. I remember the special sealed-off area with Rauli lying there on the bed. Only his hand shook and I held it. No time. The guards abruptly called, 'Quickly! Time's over; time's over!'

"We went out of the building. It was slippery outside. The guards were paranoid that I'd try to escape. I made a small movement, and the guard jumped around, coming at me, when he fell on his backside. I looked at him and said, 'Communists are going to fall on their bottoms just like you.'

"I was taken back to Katajanokka. Raul's illness affected many of the boys in jail. Paul Saar did a lot for me. He was very kind, offered comfort in a very dark, dark time. That image that I had seen in the Ratakatu jail kept coming back to me. What did this mean?"

December 7th, 1947

Dearest Fredy!

Loving wishes once again, here from home!

I just put Jyri to bed so now I have a good opportunity

to write to you, dear old man, as I wait for Kerttu. Kerttu has been here with me, faithfully, every night as well as a big part of each day. She is doing almost all the housework, even the child's laundry, as I cannot do anything. I can't concentrate on anything; my thoughts are only with little Rauli and you. I think of how matters will turn out, if you could get home, how things would work out better once more, if we could be together to share in the loss of Rauli.

Dear, let's pray ceaselessly as prayer is the only thing that can help in trouble. God will perform a miracle, so that you can get home.

Beloved, let us believe also in God's help so that you will be able to come next Sunday to send Raul to his final resting place. You know as well as I how God has helped us when we have sought his help, but how often we have forgotten Him – His great love for us!

The Lord has now tried us with little Raul's death and your imprisonment, and with all of this, He has his own good reasons, and when we get through all this with His help, then surely He will bless us and help us onward.

I was at church this morning; we gave thanks for our little Raul Juhani. Golden little Raul, how he is always everything, everywhere. No matter where I look, I see only blond-haired Rauli: there he is; his dear little being is always with me. I feel disbelief that he has died.

I spoke about the shop to Onni, Ami and Casi and everyone agreed that it is not important to think about this now. As it will not be settled soon (it won't be solved in a few weeks, as we had hoped), so we should wait until your dilemma clears and then take the shop's matters to task.

The taxes are to be paid in any case by December 22nd, but other bills can wait for now, and in my opinion, when we think correctly about it, the decision is good – isn't it so in your opinion? Nothing good will come of hasty decisions. All the work in the shop, the bills, etc. take time. Kotka's Art Club took the half-finished works and will finish them as best as they can, by themselves.

I finish for now. Kerttu already arrived and Jyri is making noises wanting to get up – he is such a lap-child!

All the best to you. Loving wishes, your small
Maire and Jyri

Now, as I read those letters of Mother's, I cry. I am there, right there, with her, back in 1947. Truly, I can smell her tears on those pages now yellowed with age, bringing to reality all that she felt, all that she was going through...

Also, continuing efforts were being made to save the Estonians from being sent to Siberia.

Helsinki newspaper, "New Finland," December 1947

"The Estonian Question Has Not Been Dealt with in Cabinet"

Yesterday, Cabinet was to deal with the matter of the Estonians held captive, but Minister of Justice Eino Pekkala told "New Finland" that he knew nothing of the matter, nor did he know whether the item could be dealt with during the absence of either of the foreign ministers (Russian and Finnish), or even whether the deportation question was going to go before Cabinet at all.

Twelve of the detainees are in the Provincial Prison,

and one is in Valpo's jail. No orders have been given at the Provincial Prison to deport the men nor has Valpo had orders to surrender them. The hearings have now been completed. The men have calmly submitted to their fate, and they have the right to meet their families as well as receive food packages. There has been no disturbance or food fasting to protest at the Provincial jail.

Our paper inquired yesterday whether or not there was truth to the information that the Minister of the Interior, Leino, would not have given the order for the detainment. Valpo's police chief Erkki Tuominen refused to comment. He only said that after twenty-three days there have been no new arrests. Special orders to cease the detainments have not been given.

In government circles, it is a widely-held belief that if an appeal was made to the ombudsman, then the matter would be clarified thoroughly. Ombudsman Mauno Laisaari agreed to the legitimacy of this and, in so doing, was also surprised that this appeal has not been made. He regarded the whole Estonian issue as a dark undertaking, which has not been given legal explanation. Appeals to him could be presented by the families of the arrested men.

"Peace Agreement's Strange Interpretation"
According to some lawyers, the treatment of the Estonians is completely contrary to what the terms of the peace agreement dictate. Under Article 7 of the agreement, it is clear that requirements are made for those types of people who have during the war been sympathetic to the Allies and their cause, and that they should be set free without delay. As the Estonians in question escaped to avoid service in the German army, this is a clear indication of their feelings against the Germans.

Father gathers some strength and continues:

"Well, then I got permission so that I could go to the funeral to bury my son. I was given my civilian clothes, taken to the Helsinki train station. Luckily, I got a kind policeman to escort me, the one who was not Communist. When he went to buy the tickets, he left me alone on the bench. I could have disappeared then. But he must have understood that I would not miss my son's funeral. We boarded the train like two gentlemen. The guard said that he had orders to handcuff me, but he wouldn't do this. He added, 'You Estonians will be freed, surely, one day.'

"During the ride, he talked about his own life, how he had been in the Winter War and been wounded. A very nice man.

"We arrived in Hamina and went to the police station. I was allowed to go home. Friends of ours arrived, expressing condolences. Covertly, words were spoken, and precise important words uttered. When Casi arrived, we were alone for a time, so were able to speak.

"In the morning, Maire's father brought the little white coffin and laid it on the white snow. It was a very cold day. There was some singing by the Hamina Male Choir. Some of the men had come to sing, but this was not in focus at the time.

"After the funeral, we had a small reception at our place. Casi Edelman and Ville Leomaki were the ones who had big plans for me. My time at home would soon be over, and the following day, I was to be escorted back to Katajanokka Prison.

"So, as planned, Edelman and Leomaki came to the reception, but left after a while.

"When my dear friends returned, they pretended they were drunk. They carried on, making quite a scene. They had a Club Seven cigarette pack, and on the back cover, drunkenly told me that I should paint a wonderful landscape, that looked like this, and this and this…It was actually a map, and while carousing, they showed me the critical points on the map. Where I was to jump, where to go. 'Yes, I'll try to paint something for you!' I joined in. Casi Edelman, particularly, played his part very well. Key words were quickly whispered.

"The kind guard came to Maire and said, 'Please Mrs. Karu, tell those men that they should leave. On such a day they dare to behave like this.' Mother knew something was in the air about plans for escape, but was not told anything more. It was better that she did not know. So she played along, and pretended to be upset at the drunken behaviour of the friends. Soon, everyone left, and Maire, Alfred, Jyri and the guard were in the house."

Maire now adds, "Father pretended that he had a horrible stomach upset, and so I had to go to the pharmacy to get some medicine. I knocked on the door of the pharmacist about five o'clock the next morning. I could see the owner was annoyed about being awakened so early. But I did everything I could to help things along. This was part of the scheme. But I knew nothing of the exact plans.

"Arriving home, I gave Alfred the medicine, and made breakfast. Everything was in a turmoil inside. Alfred and I could not speak about what was happening, only superficial things. There was Jyri, sleeping soundly in his crib, luckily.

"Soon the guard, Alfred and I walked to the train station. It was still dark outside. We said our farewells. Was I ever to see my husband again?

"The train disappeared.

"In the dark, the cold winter weather seemed even worse as I walked quickly back home to a very lonely house. Once in, I just sat on the bed and sobbed. Jyri came up to me, put his little hands around my neck. He spoke early, and he said, 'Don't cry airi, Juli here, Juli here.' We clung to each other.

Now Father continues: "I knew the place where I had to jump, and what I was to do after the jump. The train pulled away, about 6:30 a.m. I sat beside the guard, moaning about my stomach. The guard did not put the handcuffs on me this time either, which was another lucky break. I kept getting up, going to the bathroom, timing the ride all the while. Imagine the tension. I knew that I had to jump from the train at exactly 7:14, there was to be no mistake, no delay. No one could stall me; I had to be ready. The stomach upset enabled me to keep others away, without suspicion of why I was always stalling around the doors.

"Timing was crucial. The train was speeding. I saw the snowy landscape with houses dotted in the dusk. When I was to jump, I had no idea of where I was going to land, it had to be very precise. I had no jacket on, no gloves, no hat, just my suit. It was cold, dark.

"One last time, I made my way to the washroom, slipped between the doors separating each car, and jumped. I flew through the air, it seemed for only a second. After landing, the first thing I did was feel that my hands, legs, were okay. Nothing was broken. I made it.

"Getting up, I saw, just in front of me, a deep ravine. That would have been a nasty fall, had I jumped further out! But most of all, I was afraid that the train would stop. I stood there, hardly able to breathe. Had the Valpo police been on the train, the train would surely have stopped. But the train clacked on and disappeared from sight. I breathed a sigh of relief, and gave a silent heartfelt 'thank you' to the guard who I believed was on my side.

"The incredible thing is, also, that just about six inches from where I had landed, was a huge boulder. A split-second difference would have meant I would have had a rather bad crash. However, I landed in the snow. So then I got my bearings. Yes, there was the road only a few hundred yards from where I stood. I went through everything I had been told.

"Once on the road, I was to walk left, and go until I saw a house where, on the second floor, there was a single light.

"I was at the right place at the right time. Had I been a kilometre off, I would have taken the wrong point for bearings, and perhaps gone to the wrong house. Then who knows what would have happened?

"So I was lucky so far. I walked into the yard of the house. There was a taxi waiting for me. I didn't know the person in the car, didn't know if he could really be trusted. But I had no alternative. The car slowly took off, down the wintry road. We drove right back to Hamina!

"That vision I had in prison came before me many times, and I repeated, 'My son has saved me.'

"The news of my escape had reached Maire by afternoon, via a neighbour's son, who was en route to university. He had spotted a policeman walking at the Kotka station (which is about 50 km. from Hamina) carrying a man's coat and hat. The young man called his parents to tell them that he felt Karu must have escaped!"

Maire adds: "After Father left, all I could do was hope that things would turn out. There was Jyri, just a year old. I was due in a month. Rauli was gone, so was my husband. But I was not alone, as many friends kept helping, as well as dear Kerttu and my father."

"So, we got back to Hamina," continues Father. "The taxi driver took me to a building right behind the police station. That in itself was quite risky, but Casi knew what he was doing. No one would think that Karu would double-back. The search was on, but in the other direction. Casi silently walked in, greeted me, as I hid in the closet of the house. The house was owned by a friend who was very trustworthy.

"The plan was to wait so that I would go on a ship to England. Many ships, of course, used Hamina harbour. But the boys then got worried about the captain of the ship – he was an alcoholic so wasn't to be trusted. That plan was then dropped.

"I was kept hidden about a week and a half as new plans were being made. I sat in hiding, wanting very much to run home to Maire, to ease her during this time of sorrow. I knew that she had no idea where I was – it was much better that way, in case she was questioned. So close, yet so far!

"The other alternative was to get to Sweden – but how?

"My friends took me to stay at another house, this time right by the Russian border. Arrangements had been made ahead of time with the owner, and so I was secreted to the top floor of the farm house. Only the farmer knew I was there, and he would sneak food to me. I crept around upstairs, and even drew some sketches from the window. No bath, no shower, just a chamber pot up there in my hiding place. I was in this spot for a few days, and then once again, was taken away.

"The person who took over now was a man who Maire knew, a man named Pentti Taavitsainen. He would now be the guiding force. A very daring Finn, intent on helping. Look at this man. He had a family of his own. Who would have taken such a risk to help me? He was incredible. Actually, he did much to help the Estonians. The risk that he took was so high that he had to leave to go to Switzerland with his wife and children. They lived in Switzerland for about six years returning in 1954. Here was a true hero, a man whose integrity and bravery are uncommon. He went the extra distance for others.

"I was driven by another taxi to Helsinki. My life was in the hands of my trusted friends. Arriving in Helsinki, I stayed with Pentti and his wife. They lived on the main floor of a general's house. This place had a lovely sauna, as I recall. By now a month had gone by.

"New Year's Eve 1948 I will always remember. Pentti, his wife Eila, and I celebrated quietly, and we poured hot lead into cold water, a custom where luck is determined by the shapes formed.

"This would tell what kind of year lay ahead.

"That night, we also went ski jumping. Pentti was a first-rate jumper, had won Finnish National Amateur ski jumping competitions. I really wanted to go, so Pentti reluctantly agreed, giving me a pair of his skis. Off we went. The hill was lit up, so we saw where we were jumping. But I had never jumped at such a height before, and Pentti gave me some advice, demonstrating. It was wonderful, flying through the air, free, but then the landing was inevitable. My landings were really awful. I never did master that aspect of jumping!

"We enjoyed ourselves immensely and, after a few hours, made our way back to the house in the darkness. There, my thoughts again turned bleak, but I had to keep my spirits up.

"Pentti's first plan to get me out was that I go in a plane to Sweden, and then parachute off. Pentti had been a fighter pilot, and he would have flown. But the plane required clearance and of course this was too visible, might attract too much attention.

"So my dear friend then concocted the following: I became a forester named Pellervo – Pentti's brother. Pentti got false papers and passport, and so I had a new alias. Preparations were made in exact detail, so that we would be ready for anything that might happen.

"On January 8th, 1948, the two 'brothers' departed Helsinki accompanied by a driver. I was wearing a big fur coat, had a cigar in my mouth – a big shot operator, going to check out some of my forestry concerns. We had guns under the seats, just in case we would need them.

"The weather cooperated, and we drove at quite a speed to Tornio. The trip lasted about ten hours. Tornio is about 700 km. from Helsinki. Remember, in 1948 speeds were not that great, nor were the roads. We spoke of how other Estonians could be set free, whether those left in Katajanokka were still there. The small man sitting beside me was really a giant. He would do whatever he could to help the cause. We were nearing Tornio, and knew that we were almost safe. Pentti had already somehow contacted a certain border guard who knew we were coming. He greeted us and showed us where to go.

"Arriving at our destination, I got the skis out quickly, looked Pentti in the eye, thanked him. We embraced farewell. Off I went, across the Tornio River. It was of course dark, and luckily the ice was in great condition. You have never seen anyone ski so fast! Sweden, and safety, lay on the other side.

"As soon as I reached the other side, Haparanda, the Swedish Border Patrol, received me. I was cared for as though I was a small child. At Haparanda the Swedes had a refugee camp, with Finns, Estonians – men, women and children. Safety at last!

My stay at this camp was difficult, even though the care was excellent and the people were kind. My thoughts were always with the past, with Maire and Jyri – with Raul. I remember painting during this time. Clearly I still see the painting of the red Swedish house in the snow. I got money for some of my pictures. With my first money,

I bought a huge carton of oranges for everyone in the camp. There was a vitamin deficiency and, oh, the people were all so happy.

After about a month, I was able to get a contact through Casi, and I got news of Marjut's birth. Then I felt really bad."

"No, it was Pentti who contacted you," says Mother.

Father replies: "I know what happened. Don't you interfere all the time...then I got to know that I had a daughter. I was so upset: how could I have lost my wife, family, home? A heavy feeling of hopelessness came over me. I sunk into depression. So I was given some pills, some tranquillizers.

"A friend of mine was a doctor, and he was working at the hospital one night. He told me to come and see him there. I kept swallowing pills and got a pass to go to the hospital for a visit. Well, we had some pure alcohol to drink – you know, they disinfect the instruments with that stuff.

"It was awful. I hadn't told my friend that I had taken quite a few tranquillizers before. However, I made my way back to the camp. Suddenly I became a great speaker. Very intelligent, knowing everything, I woke everyone up in the camp. Yes, there I was, centrestage, my soliloquy was about life's trials, religious questions. It was about 1:00 a.m. by this time. The audience, bleary-eyed, listened quietly. The men wept. Then I passed out.

"When I awoke, I was in hospital. I had my stomach pumped. Wretched fool that I was! Mixing tranquillizers and alcohol. Now I can laugh about this, but at the time I was in despair.

"Day-to-day life at the camp was fine. The chief of police had a birthday, I think it was his fortieth. I was asked to paint a portrait of him, and this turned out quite well.

"Everyone at the camp was asked about what kind of work they could do. I said I could do picture framing; this was all linked to my artistic life, and my little business back in Hamina.

"The Swedish government really helped us. We were given food, clothing, jobs. Exceptional.

"So after spending a few weeks at the refugee camp, I was sent to Tranos. When I got off the train, a man came towards me, greeted me:

"Sprechen sie Deutsch?" We spoke in German, as I knew very little Swedish. He told me that there were quite a few Estonians already in Tranos. The man who greeted me was to become my employer and friend. Accommodations were arranged, and I lived in a house with another Estonian fellow, in Sommen, which was about a half-hour train ride from Tranos.

"Estonian Independence Day, February 24th, 1948, I met other Estonians at a hall. Sure, Estonia was still our country in our hearts. We would continue to celebrate its independence, forever hoping! We organized a lovely affair, and it was good to be able to converse once again in Estonian. Here I met Dr. Arnold Laansoo and his family, the Luides, Toomsalus and Oedermaas.

"During all this time, I had a code name, 'Mimosa.' This was used by contacts in Finland. All information I sent back was under 'Mimosa.' Mimosa means 'sensitive plant' – having complex fern-like leaves that, in some species, are sensitive to touch or to changes in light and temperature. In my predicament, I was indeed sensitive to many outside influences!

"I wrote Maire some letters, addressing the letters to Pentti, using my code name. Pentti would take the letters directly to Maire."

Maire adds, "Yes, I would read the letters and then throw them into the fire right away all winter and spring. Marjut, now don't write this down, no names of people who helped. We don't want this."

"Why? Nothing is going to happen; it's been over fifty years now, Mother," I reply.

"Well, still, all kinds of books have been written and also Viirlaid wrote the one about us *Markitud* (*Branded*). No, no, we just want the memoir to be more about Father's art life."

"That's kind of boring," I say.

"No, it's not. Just don't write any of this other part down."

I ignore Mother and wonder why, then, did they talk to me about all these things? The reason for writing this down was just to remember things as they were!

But I notice that Father does not agree with Mother, simply because he doesn't say anything, avoiding conflict. This is my signal to go ahead.

I know that Mother would prefer to recount everything in a happier light, looking at their lives with rosy recollections. Still, she has been willing to tell me most of what she could remember. Privately, she is willing to say more, but is worried about things that would be written down. Throughout the years, I have known that there was always a dread in our house, of people knowing about Father's escape, of somehow feeling that he could still be taken back, or that his children could still be made to suffer.

Now, we have come this far, my parents are in their seventies. The situation in Russia has changed, and in Estonia.

"Father, tell me what was happening in Sweden…"

"Well, I got a job in a picture frame factory. The man who met me at the train station was Mr. Helberg, and I worked hard and got a pretty good reputation. Also, I designed different new frames. When Mr. Helberg found out I was also an artist, he had an altogether different face. "You can take time off to go and paint! We can arrange an art exhibition!" The man was wonderful and very supportive of my art. Now Mr. Helberg's framing business is one of Europe's biggest.

"So, I worked and also painted. What I painted I sold immediately. I even got the frames for free from Mr. Helberg.

"Keeping busy, trying to get some money so that if and when my family could join me, I would have something to offer, helped me through the months of loneliness."

"Mother, how did you manage back in Hamina, when Father left?"

"Oh, ya, before you were born, Marjut, things in our lives were relatively normal."

"What, does this mean that after I was born, things would be abnormal?" I laugh. Mother didn't mean it that way!

"Well, Father left, and all I knew was that he had escaped. I received no news but lived in hope that soon some good news would come, that we could get in contact.

"When Father left, I had to get a cheaper apartment, so we moved to a smaller place. We had three big windows in our living room and I kept the curtains open most of the time. One night, my father came to visit us, and when he entered he whispered that we were being watched. There was a man standing almost directly under our windows at the front. I realized with a sudden fear that I had been watched for some time.

"One day the Communist policeman who lived close by came right into my kitchen. He said, 'Your husband has escaped.' I had a dustpan and broom in my hand, sweeping the kitchen floor when he entered. I then gave the best performance of my life. I sank into a chair, clasped my hand to my heart, and stuttered, 'Wha...what – is this possible? When?'

"'Calm down, calm down, dear lady, surely your husband is already safely on the Swedish side.' I pretended I was in shock – quite a good act."

Now as I look at Mother's old scrap book, I read an old newspaper clipping from the Hamina Daily Newspaper:

December 14th, 1948

"OUR FRIEND IS IN NEED"

For known reasons, artist Alfred Karu has not been able to keep up with his art and framing business and his family is undergoing hardship. Help them so they can get on their feet! At M. Ulander's home, there will be a sale of the artist's valuable works just in time for that Christmas gift. "Oy Laatulelu" has generously offered to frame any works, so act quickly so you will have your art framed for that Christmas gift. Go at your earliest convenience, and also look at the selection of frames and bring your other framing in as soon as possible.

Then another article which reads:

"We Meet on the Street"

An active family woman, Mrs. E. Puhakka, who is a close member of artist Alfred Karu's circle of friends, along with acquaintances, is organizing a drive for donations for this young Estonian and his family, who have suffered much and are undergoing hardship. We understand that artist Karu is being held by the Valtio police, though last Sunday he was allowed, under police guard, to attend his son's funeral. Mrs. Puhakka stated, "The death of their son is another hard blow, which increased the already difficult situation." So friends got together and thought of how they could help. "The best way, we thought, was by giving the family money so a drive was started."

We were curious to know how this drive was coming along, and asked Mrs. Puhakka to elaborate. "The people in Hamina have wanted to help and the response has been incredible. I would say almost unbelievable. People have opened their wallets as soon as they have seen the donation list. This is not an official drive, but we – the friends – wanted to help in some way, to make their lives better. We felt that the best way was with a money gift. Already we have been able to give Mrs. Karu enough money so that she can pay her necessary bills. But she will soon have an additional child; this will take a large portion of the money collected. Our work, therefore, is not over yet. Also I have heard that artist Karu's framing shop will be reopened, and it is my opinion that this is very important, as the family has had many expenses and the shop could pay some of the bills. Furthermore the business can help heal the wounds."

So, we were a family in need! This I never knew! Well, let's continue with Mother's tale:

"On Tuesday January 20th, I went to see my father at Pitajansaari. I stayed the night with Jyri. My father and Saimi made up a story that they had to go to Helsinki to visit the two aunts. They needed to see them, I was told. Later I found out from Aunt Edla that Father had gone to Helsinki to pay all the debts from getting Fredi out. The taxi drivers, even the people in Tornio, had to be paid. Of course, Pentti never wanted anything but, justifiably, the others had to be paid. They too had taken great risks. My father and another person in Hamina paid everything. It was a lot of money. My father never told me this. He was a very quiet and kind man.

"While at home, I told Kerttu that I did not want to go to Kotka to have the baby. I felt very alone and lonely. This baby would be born at home. So, the next morning Jyri and I went back home to Hamina, and Kerttu went to inform the midwife. Kerttu stayed the night with us, and on January 22nd, the labour pains started. The midwife was fetched, and she was wonderful. She told me about her own little girl, whose name was Marjut. All went well, and a baby girl was born at 1:40 p.m. 'I would be very honoured if you would name your baby Marjut,' said the midwife.

"'That is just what I was thinking,' I replied. So, Marjut Heljo Tuulikki was the name chosen. Heljo was the name her father would have wanted.

"January 22nd was also the day that the Estonians were to be sent to Russia, and I was very anxious about this. Kerttu brought me every paper, and I stayed up two nights, not sleeping. Yes, I knew that Fredy was not at Katajanokka Prison, but where was he? Was he in some other jail, or was he safe? All I knew was that friends were trying to help him.

"Marjut was born on the Thursday, and on the following Monday there was a knock at the door. Kerttu answered. I heard her telling the visitor that Maire was not able to greet anyone; she was in bed. The insistent man said that he had to see Maire; it was of some importance. So Kerttu let him in. There was Pentti, an old school friend of mine. Pentti came to my bedside and said, 'Alfred is safe. He sends his greetings.'

"I stared at the man, and started to tremble, then to cry. 'How do you know? What do you know?' I blurted out.

"'I accompanied Fredy to Tornio – I cannot say more than this, but he is safe, trust me,' he answered. What wonderful news! Up until then, I did not know for certain if Fredy indeed had escaped to safety. So he was in Sweden now. 'We, of course, must not mention this to anyone but our trusted friends, and we shall be quiet about all of this,' said Pentti. The man's visit was short; he had to get back to Helsinki, but had come to visit me. Miracles were taking place! How could we ever repay these kind people?

"Well, now all we had to do was wait, bide our time, and see when things could be arranged for correspondence.

"There I was, with Jyri clinging to me, and the little baby in her basket.

"See, no one, including me, knew what was happening with Fredy, except for the three friends. It was an extremely sensitive issue and great caution was essential. Even the wives of the men who helped Fredi escape didn't know anything. The whole thing was very well organized. If the men would have been found out, they would have been sent to Russia.

"You understand, even up until 1989, I was afraid to even write letters to certain people…

"We were also worried about the futures of these men. They were heroes certainly!

"As it turned out, Pentti had to leave Finland in any case. He was taken in for questioning, and for the safety of his family, he moved to Switzerland, as Father said.

"I read the newspapers constantly, and the story of the Estonians was certainly now front page material" (*Helsingin Sanomat*).

"Outcome for the Estonians Decided"
Thirty to Be Handed over to Russia
The Government, after long deliberation, made a decision regarding the Estonians held in prison for four

months. The Finnish government will give thirty of these men to the Russians: they are seen as prisoners of war, having fought against the Russian Army. The grounds for this decision hinged on the terms of the peace agreement, under Article 9B.

So, even after all the work and intervention, even of other countries, Finland was in the strong hold of Communists who ran the show. ...

A few days later, in a Helsinki paper:

"Dramatic Escape Attempted!"
Four men tried to Escape – Caught by Prison Guards
The handing over of the Estonians took place this morning at Vainikka border station at about 6 a.m. Finnish officials gave the fifteen Estonians and fifteen other war prisoners back to Russian officials. These men had been held four months in Helsinki's Provincial Prison, Katajanokka.

The families of the prisoners were allowed to visit yesterday, taking supplies, clothes and food to their loved ones. Many of the prisoners are married to Finns, and these young couples have small children. The parting was not easy. Other Estonians living in Helsinki went to see the men as well, giving each of them a parcel of food.

Before the Estonians were sent off yesterday, a dramatic escape was attempted. This happened at the Katajanokka Prison, during the time when the prisoners were allowed out of their cells for a walk out in the prison yard. Our information is that when the prisoners were about to be taken back to their cells, four men slipped past the guards and ran for the prison gates, about one hundred feet away. The guards immediately turned, but couldn't reach the men in time, as they had forced the guard at the gate to give the keys. Opening the gate, the men rushed out onto Vyo Street, running off. The guards chased the men, as the prisoners slipped past a few pedestrians. The guards shot at the escapees; the shots could be heard for some distance. A witness told the paper that the guards nearly shot at innocent pedestrians on the street, and one woman was heard screaming, "Don't shoot me!" According to an eye witness, the guards soon caught two of the prisoners right on Vyo Street and the third was apprehended in a nearby yard. The fourth man managed to make it down to the corner of Vy and Laivasto Street, hopped over a railing there, near the Officer's Building.

Another eyewitness, dressed in civilian clothes, had seen a man running, so had then hidden in a corner of an entrance way, with his pistol ready, waiting for the running prisoner. This passerby happened to be an off-duty police officer in civilian clothes. He thought the culprit trying to escape was a regular convict. The fugitive had jumped onto a horse, which was pulling a sleigh, heading towards the centre of town. The alert policeman managed to run and stop the horse, by firing a shot towards it. He also then shot at the prisoner. The guards arrived on the scene and reporters were told that another shot would have been fired if necessary...Ilmar Mannik received a slight wound to his left arm, and after this, all was quiet.

We have been told that another Estonian tried to escape last Wednesday morning, when two Estonians were transported to the hospital for health reasons. On the way back, one of the men, Sirel, tried to escape, eluding the guards, but a few shots were fired at him, and he was caught as well. Sirel is an engineer, who worked for some time for the Finnish National Radio.

At the prison yard, inside the gates, at exactly 5 p.m. yesterday, four big prison trucks and five passenger cars, many policemen and guards assembled for the transfer. A few women tried to get in through the gates, carrying parcels, but they were stopped. The trucks and cars waited a few minutes and some loud commands could be heard in the prison yard. The prisoners, now in civilian clothes, were marched in rows to the waiting vehicles. The men were handcuffed, each holding a bag or small suitcase in their constrained hands.

The first prison truck, known by police as "Black Mary" filled with eight passengers and many armed guards. This truck left with a car following it, along Kauppia Street, then turned the corner, out of sight. Altogether, four prison trucks with heavily armed guards left the gates of the prison towards the train station, with five cars following.

Everything went smoothly and peacefully. Just before 5 p.m., a small group of policemen gathered to oversee that the prisoners were boarded on to a special secured boxcar that was on the side tracks of the station.

People at the station at this time were unaware of the proceedings, as the prison car was secured in a corner of the railway yard, on the side tracks, away from the regular area. At five p.m., the first "Black Mary" arrived, followed by the car. But the policeman in the first car didn't have the keys to the prison boxcar, so had to wait for the arrival of the next truck and car. As well as the guards and police, a plain clothes officer representing the government held a machine gun. A police officer then read from a list the names of the men in the first truck and they were then moved onto the boxcar. After the first truck was unloaded, the same was done with the following trucks. The guards and police formed a chain surrounding the prisoners as they were escorted out. Behind this stood reporters. The only disruption to the proceedings came when a young man, who, at the door of the boxcar, turned abruptly and with a loud clear voice shouted, "Long live Finland!" The police didn't miss a beat and continued with the reading of the names. One prisoner, Mannik, was without handcuffs as his arm was bandaged from the wound suffered from the morning's attempted escape.

After the loading of the prisoners, a truck drove up and unloaded boxes and some suitcases into the boxcar.

It was learned that engineer Sirel's parents had telegraphed to inform their son that they had received permission to travel from Estonia to Leningrad to greet him there.

Later that evening, at about 11:15 p.m., hundreds of people had arrived at the Helsinki train station, thinking that the prisoners were to leave then on an express train to Savonlinna. Police were stationed at the railway building and asked the people to show their boarding tickets, but nonetheless, the crowd stayed. The last car of this express train was sealed, with closed curtains, and this is where the crowd gathered. But this was not the Estonian car after all. The prisoners' train had left earlier, at 5:30 p.m., to Kerava, and from there, on to Savonlinna via an earlier express train.

About thirty policemen tried to peacefully disperse the upset crowd that now scattered to see the other cars of the train. In the crowd were the families of the Estonian men. They had come in vain. The prisoners were already en route to Savonlinna to the border station in Vainikka. Here they were handed over to the Russians, at about 6 a.m. this morning.

Another prisoner, who had been detained since November, artist Alfred Karu, had escaped when Valpo allowed him to attend his son's funeral.

Fifteen other prisoners-of-war who were from Inkeri, Russia, and one from Latvia, were handed over, along with the fifteen Estonians.

Yes, that day, hundreds crowded at the Helsinki train station to see the men off. Pentti had plans to save the other Estonians who were being sent to Siberia from Katajanokka Prison. He had exact plans ready, to seize the guards, take the men. But someone must have smelled something, as that day the boys were taken to that other area ready for shipment out, hours earlier. Those boys lost their chance for freedom and went to Siberia.

Among those on that train was Paul Saar. He would do time in Siberia, sit in prison camps, questioned and tried. His faith was a shining light to him. He recounted how once, sitting in a tiny cell, he had peered out through a small crack in the wooden wall and saw a church spire. This for him was an inspiring, wonderful sight giving him hope and strength. Paul was separated from his Finnish wife and little son. Because Paul was a pastor, he therefore was seen as speaking against communist beliefs and so was punished more for this as well. He kept giving little services, even while doing time in mines shovelling coal.

Paul would meet his son, Pekka, when Pekka was a grown man. Paul's wife was killed in a traffic accident when Pekka was twelve, leaving him virtually an orphan. His father was separated from him by the Iron Curtain.

Fifty years later, when we met Reverend Saar here in Toronto, I was immediately drawn to him. One could feel the glow of human kindness and empathy for the human condition when looking at this remarkable man. He recounted the day in 1948 that the prisoners were taken, travelling in boxcars to the Russian border. He remembered how one boy had a knife, and had desperately cut, cut, into the wooden planks of the train, only to hit steel. There, his hopes ended. Though Pastor Saar was devastated to part with his wife and young son, his outlook was that God had a reason for this and He had a plan for him.

When the Pastor sat at our home all those years later, he was looking at some of our old pictures and saw one of Raul. He said, "And yes, here is the little Raul, who saved your life, Alfred."

The calling for Pastor Saar led him to do a lot of work with the people who were from Inkeri, a zone taken by the Russians. He lived and worked with the poor, hungry and destitute. Today, Paul lives happily near Tallinn with his second wife. His daughter and her young family live in Tartu. Paul often sees his son Pekka, who is a neurologist in Helsinki. The story of Paul's trials were written in a book, called *Toinen Vyottaa Sinut* (*Another Will Gird You – Paul Saar's Road to the Ministry in Estonia and in Inkeri*, written by Martti Issakainen.)

But now, back to Maire there in Hamina...

"Yes, this is the way it was. I read every paper and was very frustrated, couldn't believe that the government would let the men go."

Another article appeared in February 1948:

"Who Will Care for the Families?"

The families of the men sent to Russia are now without the heads of the households and many are now destitute. Their case had been brought before the government, but under the agreement with Russia, it is understood that marriages between Finns and Estonians, and the Inkeri people, should be forbidden. The Russian viewpoint is that these marriages are invalid.

When the list was read yesterday of the prisoners to be sent, the good news arrived for four men who had been detained for many months awaiting decision on their fate. These four were set free, as they were not wanted by the Russian government.

Mother goes on: "Life in Hamina was bearable. I had wonderful support from my family and our friends.

"In February, Inna Pyykonen, Paavo's wife (Paavo the artist), came over to visit, and left in the early evening. I was getting the dishes cleared, when Inna reappeared at the door about a half-hour later. 'Maire, Paavo has just come back from Helsinki and there he saw a disturbing thing. He met a Finnish lady with her little girl – but she was married to a man from Inkeri (that part of Finland that was taken by the Russians, on the eastern border). She had been detained and her daughter was to be sent to Russia just because her father was now seen as a Russian!'

"I almost dropped the cup I was putting away. My heart started to beat quickly. Now the scare was that the children with an Estonian parent would be sent to Russia. As Alfred was now technically a Russian, his children were seen as such. These were the stories that we now began to hear.

"We became quite frightened and so our friends decided to arrange for an immediate departure for the children and me to Sweden. Certainly we could not risk the children being taken!

"I hadn't even had Marjut christened yet. I had to go and talk to my father. Inna stayed with the children and I bundled up, took off in the middle of the night with the kick sled. There must have been sparks flying behind me. I went as fast as I could to Pitajansaari. I banged on Father's door.

"Once again poor Father was up all night while we discussed what we should do. Certainly everything must be done so that the children would not be taken. He agreed that if things could be arranged safely I should leave. Pentti took a great risk again, quickly organizing yet another exit.

"I left my father and took off to see the Edelmans. I woke them up and told them about my departure. 'But we need to christen Marjut before we leave!' So Casi said he'd go and meet the pastor first thing in the morning and bring him to our home.

"At nine, sure enough, in came the pastor, the Edelmans, Kerttu, my father and Saimi. I had been up all night packing and hadn't slept at all.

"Our train was leaving at about noon for Tornio. I don't know where I got any money – Father probably gave some to me. Yes, Father gave it to me.

"So the baptism was held. The Edelmans and Kerttu were the godparents. We used that antique crystal bowl, which we still have, for the water. The bowl is well over a hundred years old. We used this same bowl for Raul and Jyri. Marjut had no christening gown, only her swaddling clothes. We had no coffee, only that korviketta – substitute coffee made from grain. No cakes, no time for anything but to get everything ready to go.

"But suddenly, a very strong feeling of peace came over me. I felt that everything would work out well for us, that we should stay. Just like that, I decided to stay, telling my friends that no, I am staying. We unpacked all the things.

"We tried to make a celebration of the christening, now that we had more time. But I could see that my father and others had worried looks on their faces. What more? Marrying an Estonian had certainly brought its share of troubles.

"From then on I took extreme care. I kept the curtains on the street side of the house tightly shut, always had the doors locked. I didn't go out for some time. The children were inside. I really didn't let them out of my sight. Kerttu and Father brought groceries. Friends and family had their own special knock so that I knew I could open the door.

"Gradually, I became more bold, and just had a feeling that we would be alright, no harm would come to us.

"We received two packages of coffee and a package of oranges from Sweden. These were sent to us by Hannes Oja. Hannes had left for Sweden right after the war ended. He had been at our engagement party and, of course, knew all about those letters Fredy and I were exchanging at that time. I don't know how Hannes got our address, but oh, when the first package arrived, it was incredible: blood oranges and some coffee. After all these years, his kindness still touches me.

"So I stayed on in Hamina, didn't let anyone in who I didn't know, certainly not the policeman. But I was always on guard. In April, Pentti let me know where I could reach 'Mimosa' so I wrote him a letter.

April 27th, 1948

Hamina

My own love!
How unspeakably hard it must be for you, dear, to be waiting for news from here – needlessly not knowing how we, at this end, are doing. And how earnestly day to day I have awaited a letter from there, even though I know this is not possible. However, I still hope for the sake of hoping.

On both sides there are difficulties, no matter how much I wish to write hundreds of lines, even volumes.

In the end, I now dare to write. The main thing is that you, dearest, are fine and knowing this I can happily await that day when everything is like before and hopefully even better, at least this is what in my heart I hope and believe.

Dear, let's believe and trust in the Lord and ask for His help, so that he guides everything well and that he looks after us, as He has done to this point. It is remarkable when I think of it, how our all-powerful

God has guided our lives – we His weak and poor children. He loves us, even though we have so often sinned against Him. Let's leave everything in His care as he will surely guide our path.

Dear, forever-mine, how unspeakably I miss you, Fredy, my love. But I can bear everything, as I am in an altogether different position than your fellow countrymen.

Dear, I would have so much to tell you, that I wouldn't even know how to begin. There is so much happening here with all the family. I could write you a book!

First, we are well. On January first we moved to a smaller place – one room plus kitchen. This isn't at all bad, small though, and the rent is cheap: 315 markkas per month. It's on Mannerheimintie 7.

The food situation is currently quite good. We get 1.5 kg. of sugar per person per month and 1 kg. of butter. There is food as long as the money lasts. And even on that count, I am making out. When I am in real need, then help is near. I have received gifts, sold some paintings and frames, etc. So I have gone on, one day to the next.

I've received two packages from America from unknown people. Isn't it touching? I tried to hold back my tears when I received these, but I guess I cried anyway. Everyone has been so magnificent towards us, it seems like a dream.

And how about the package from the Kivinens! You should have seen Jyri's expression and how he wanted to taste those candies. That boy already understands what's good. He has become a "big boy," getting into all kinds of mischief. He is a pretty funny fellow and a great talker. Do you know what Jyri's favourite toy is? It's the painting board, the same one that little Raul played and painted on. So now Jyri paints, holding the brushes and pencils in his hand.

It was very touching for me when Jyri's first word after "mamma, pappa" was "aulu." (taulu – "painting" – without the "p"). Without any coaching! He was sitting on my lap one day and then pointed to a painting and said "aulu."

No matter where we visit, sure enough, Jyri immediately checks out all the paintings on the walls.

And how about our miss, Marjut Heljo Tuulikki. She is already three months old. She smiles a lot and is good, just like a doll, so cute in her basket.

So dear, don't worry about us; we have been getting along well.

The shop is closed. Father paid the bank loan and all other things are in order as well. Father has been incredibly supportive.

My, my, how much I would have to write to you, but I must end now, otherwise the envelope will be too bulky and it may draw attention.

Dear, in three days it is our engagement anniversary. I think back four years, how much has happened in these years – love, joy and sorrow. They say that after the rain comes sunshine and I try to believe this, even after everything we've been through.

Fredi, words cannot express how beloved you are and when I think of this I feel my heart will overflow out of my chest, when I have my own dear Fredi.

Jyri and Marjut-Heljo I love and I live for them. As well as darling little Raul there under the grass, the child who, with his life, saved his father's. That dear little child who I miss so terribly.

This time that we have lived through has taught us a lot – also it is said that nothing happens without a reason. If we wouldn't have had these trials, then we no doubt wouldn't have been able to cherish each other, valued each other.

It is late at night as I write. It is very peaceful. Only the ticking of the clock and the children's even breathing disturb the complete silence.

My thoughts drift to you: what are you doing; are you sleeping now, as it's 11:15?

It feels so sweet to let my thoughts turn to you and to imagine that I am beside you, and I can put my head against your chest and feel the big, sacred love, which the Lord has given us.

I am probably a little silly, as I sleep wearing your pyjama top, so that I may dream of you. When I put the top on, I feel that you are right here beside me.

Now I am going to sleep and to dream of you.

Fredi, my love, my own "old man," I send you bunches of greetings and many sweet kisses.

Good night, dearest! Hopefully everything will work out well! May God keep watch over you!

With much longing,
Maire, Jyri and Marjut-Heljo

P.S. Elsa's address is…Stockholm. Get in touch with her in Stockholm. I sent her some books.

April 29th, 1948

Hamina

My own dear Fredi!

Dear darling Fredi, I wrote to you the other day addressing the envelope to the factory, but I added Stockholm as I didn't know where this place, Tranos, was. Today I found out that it is a tiny little town. So if the other letter doesn't get to you, inquiries from Stockholm could be made. It is addressed to the factory but your name is then inside the envelope.

Now I have an opportunity to write through someone else, so I once again write a few words.

By the way, have your received a letter from Pentti? He was to write to you and ask for an invitation from someone there, so that I could be invited for a summer visit. He has, by the way, been training hard as he is leaving next month on the tenth, for Switzerland, and by then, he should have all those good things in order, so we shall see.

Here, life goes on quietly, but I am very lonely for you, dearest. But let's continue to trust and believe in God, so that things will go well – as long as we know how to pray and ask Him for guidance. He steers us, so that we do not keep sinning in our old ways.

Jyri boy is quite the fine "uncle" (seta). Today he was at Kaarina's playing and the dolls and carriage pleased him. He likes books a lot, every day when he escapes from my sight, then the shelves empty of books, dishes come down from the cupboards, even the flour packages are lined up on the floor, so there is a lot of hustle and bustle here every day.

The other morning he snuck into the baby's basket and sat, quite satisfied with himself, on the baby's stomach. And the poor little girl just stared. So, even this kind of thing can happen. By the way, they have been healthy all winter, no colds or coughs.

Last Monday they both got the Calmet injection against tuberculosis. Jyri has also been inoculated against whooping cough. I have tried to look after the children as well as possible, so that you, dear, would have no complaints.

Listen, go and greet Mimosa. I'll send him some

newspapers even. Now I won't write anymore; I have to go and get the forms filled out.

All the best to you and try to feel better than others. One sweet kiss for you!

Yours forever, Maire.

P.S. Elsa Lukka's address:
...Contact her!

"The month passed, and already it was approaching May. I had not heard anything from Fredy, not one letter. Trying to remain calm, I went about the daily chores, looked after the children, wondering when arrangements would be made so that we could leave the country."

May 1st, 1948
Hamina

My own dear heart!

Today, four years ago, you, dear, slid an engagement ring on my finger and sealed it with a tender kiss.

That May Day (Vappu) was the happiest and nicest May Day I ever had. Do you remember what fun we had – oh, oh, you! Dearest, how you made my head spin! How I was envied and how in love I was, as I knew I had the best man in all the world.

From all this, four years have passed into which a lot has happened. There has been joy and sunshine as well as sorrow and tears, but these have strengthened and ripened our love. You are still the same dream person now as you were then. I love you with all my heart.

Dearest, dearest, how I miss you!

Dear, how have you spent May Day? Remember to be faithful; I know my Fredi is. So, dear, do you still love me like I love you? What a lot I have to talk to you about but we'll talk, if God grants us that happiness and also that once again we can be together – the whole family. And the father can see his little children...Jyri who is such a "paappa," my, how often I laugh because of him. Even today, he was splendid when we were at Maire and Casi's for lunch. So, and also little Heljo who has never seen her father, nor her father seen her. She is, by the way, just like Raul, so alike in looks, smiling and babbling a lot already.

Yes, they give me such joy, that I cannot describe it in words. Always when I am doing things with them, or look at them, I think, "If only their father could see them now, if only he could be here now..."

Listen now, darling, I have an important matter. You must now, immediately, when you receive this letter, act in haste.

I must, for the passport application, get an invitation from a Swede, requesting us to come for summer holidays. You cannot invite, but quickly go and ensure that someone else does, a Swede. The invitation letter must also clearly state that the person will pay for all travel and expenses while there, as well as being able to meet us in Stockholm on arrival.

If the person is not well-known, then a further affidavit is needed from the police authorities, showing that he/she is capable of looking after us while we are in Sweden.

Also in the invitation it could state, for example, that they would like the children and myself to recuperate and rest, due to moving to a smaller place, and also the children could get more fruits, which we can't get here, or that their children (if any) could play with our children. The letter doesn't have to be long, just to the point.

When you get this letter try to IMMEDIATELY get the invitation and that the person sends it directly to me.

Dearest, now I end this and hope with all my heart that everything will be arranged.

Try to act as fast as possible. All the best, trusting that the Lord guides these things to a happy conclusion!

Impetuously I kiss you.

Your wife forever,
Maire

May 3rd, 1948
Hamina

Dearest, my all!

Again and again my thoughts speed to you and I again write as I got your address.

I have written three letters to you before, dear, have you received them? I addressed them to the factory. (They are very important.)

Dear, how have you been and have you been painting a lot? Ensio was here and he asked me to send you greetings and all good wishes!

We are doing well and have been healthy. I was ill earlier, but got some strong medicine from the doctor, and am now feeling fine. But it is no surprise, after all that we have been through, that I wouldn't feel so well.

I am worried about you. How you are doing, as you were not well in the fall? Try to get your strength up and don't worry at all about us.

Take care of yourself; go to the doctor so you can get some medicine to strengthen yourself so that you will get back to your old great shape.

Dear, try now as quickly as possible, to get the arrangements in order. Get in touch with Elsa; she will surely advise you if things don't get going any other way. But I believe that things will work out, as surely there are other Swedes like her.

Dear, write and ask me if I have received any letters from "Mirja-Liisa Koponen, Hamina Post Office." I shall go then and see if any have arrived.

But if the Swedish invitation arrives, then the whole thing will be clear. I'll know you've received my letters.

I end now, so that I can go and give some food to the girl, then I can get some sleep. It's already 10:30 p.m.

Goodbye my dear!

Your ever-loving girl, Mirja

Pentti was true to his word, and wrote to Alfred:

May 10th, 1948

Dear Friend,

Thank you for your letter, which I received a few days ago, to which I now reply. I am working on that invitation!

I will also be passing through Sweden and leave here on May the 20th, arriving in Stockholm on the 21st. We shall be there all day, staying at one of the following hotels: either the Wasa, Astor or Central. On Sunday evening I continue on the Nordexpress to Switzerland. The train leaves in the evening – I can't remember exactly, but it is around 10 p.m. I shall arrive at 5 a.m. in Malmo.

It would be extremely nice to meet you, but let's try to get the invitation arranged so that it arrives here in Hamina. Until we meet again, in hopes,

Pena
Hope the fountain pen works well!

May 11ᵗʰ, 1948

Dear Fredi!

Many loving greetings to you from the kitchen table, where I sit and write. Ami and Mirkku just left (it's 11:05 p.m.) as well as Kyllikki. You probably don't remember her – she was on the same train as you, back in October. She has been in Sweden, looking for you – in vain! It is incredibly nice that friends keep remembering to call on me often, so I am not alone with my thoughts too much, as Jyri and Marjut are not yet in that way company.

But how difficult and lonely I would be if I didn't have those dear golden ones as, when I am busy with them, then all the badness of the world is forgotten. Sometimes when everything feels gloomy, I need nothing more than Jyri holding me around my neck and Marjut's smile. Then everything feels easier.

Every day, from 9 to 11 a.m. and 2 to 4 p.m. Jyri plays in the park. There is a lady who looks after the children there (puisto tati), a sandbox and ten other little children about the same age. And how food and sleep taste good after being so busy.

On Sunday, Mother's Day, I went to Raul and Mother's grave with Jyri. We took flowers. We went with Henry as he now bought his own car. The whole Malinen family was along; I would not have been able to go just with Jyri.

Last year on Mother's Day Rauli was sick and now he sleeps there beside Mother. Beloved Raul and beloved Mother.

How incredible our life is: here we are today and know nothing of tomorrow. May little Raul be our guiding star and life's direction to that glorious Heaven, which in any case awaits us, if only we could remain faithful to the Lord, who directs all on earth, as we live and as we die. Nothing happens without His knowing.

Parson Ansten came to see us on Sunday as well.

Otherwise we have been well.

On Ascension Day I attended Lapinsara's twenty-fifty anniversary concert. The church was full.

Pena (Pentti) came here last night and wrote you that letter. He is leaving on the 20th and will be in Stockholm on the 21st. Try to meet him as he will be staying at one of those hotels; they are all right near the station. So, if you have any chance at all, go and meet him.

I have been waiting anxiously for that invitation, as it would have been good if I could have been able to spend summer there. Now try and get this as quickly as possible.

I have written you four letters earlier – have you received them? Have you met with Elsa yet? Inna (Pyykkonen) is also coming to Sweden the beginning of next month – if only I too could come then!

Write to me, Mirja-Liisa Koponen, Hamina Post Office, so that I will know if you got my letters and so forth.

I would like to send you some books but am still uncertain of the address. I have bought you a few art books. I just went and looked at the children. They had kicked their blankets off, as is their usual custom.

Father was here today. He will pay the bank loan this week. He is immensely helpful and good. We surely must repay him in some way, since he is giving us such a gift! I have told you, I am sure, that the shop is now closed and now there is a sewing machine shop there.

Kerttu still has no employment, and with her asthma being so bad all winter, she can't really do much. Saimi has also been sick a long time. She goes from doctor to doctor. After a bad cold she has had an infection in her sinuses, which will take some time to get over. So dear Father's life doesn't seem to be too easy.

I would have so much to tell you, but I guess I must stop now, get to sleep, as tomorrow night Suoma and Ville are coming over and I want to be a little more perky.

Dearest, I wish you all the best "why so dear you are to me!" – you know that Estonian song. You don't know how I love the Estonian language. Always when I go to Pitajansaari, I immediately turn the radio on to listen to the Estonian channel.

Goodnight my own dear man!

Try to arrange all those things that I have written to you about.

Your Maire

Maire kept waiting, every day going to the post office to see if anything had arrived for her, under the name of Mirja-Liisa Koponen…

May 12th, 1948

My dearest!

A great joy fills my heart – I received your letter today, dear. You don't know what this means to me – I have read it many, many times and then read it again. I write to you now only a short letter as your Maire is a little sick – the flu. I have to go to bed; I can't stay up.

I have had to cancel Suoma's and Ville's visit here today. Don't worry, I am sure I'll feel better by tomorrow!

I will explain everything in detail sometime when we meet. Now I end this, darling. I'll write more when I feel better. I hope you're feeling better than others!

Loving greetings to daddy, from all of us.

Maire

"After reading Alfred's letter many times, I burned it, fearing that any letters may be found out. No evidence should be left that could show that I was in contact with Alfred. So, none of the letters remain that Alfred sent me.

"Soon, an invitation arrived from Clary Faxen. Clary was a woman who Alfred got to know in Tranos, a friend of people in need! She invited the children and me to come to Sweden for a three-week vacation: this would be a wonderful holiday! Never was there any mention of Alfred, carefully avoiding his name.

"Straightaway, I took the letter of invitation to the government offices in Kotka, so that I could get the necessary passport. I was afraid I would be turned down for a pass, worried that the Karu name was still too known. But luckily the documents came through, surely sliding nicely through some bureaucrat's hands.

"Then I started to prepare for departure, secretly. No one knew except very close friends and my family. I knew that when I left, I was never coming back.

"Still, we didn't know what day the departure would be.

"On June 13th, at 5:30 a.m., we boarded the bus, leaving behind Hamina, my life, my roots. The day we left, the flowers were still on the table, my whole household remained. I only took summer clothes for all of us – nothing wintry. I was going on "vacation" but it was my exit out, towards the man I loved, for a future together.

"I only carried one big bag and Marjut had a blue pillow – don't you still have that pillow? The one with the little puppies on it? Yes, I made it into a sofa pillow. That was your pillow. In those days you couldn't get money exchanged if you were travelling – no foreign currency. But my father had managed to get me some Swedish krons through the black market. I think it was about 95 krons. I sewed this money into Marjut's pillow. This is why even today we joke about Marjut being very careful with money – it all started when we left Finland, she with the money under her head! I also crocheted around the pillow with some green yarn.

"Anyway, we stayed in Helsinki the night, at Aunt Edla's. She bathed Marjut the last night we were in Finland. Marjut's pacifier was left at her apartment, which she kept in a covered china dish for decades. I think you saw Aunt Edla, didn't you, Marjut?"

"Yes, I remember that pacifier! On my honeymoon to Finland in 1969, we visited great Aunt Edla, and she took the pacifier out of the antique dish. As she did so, the old soother crumbled," I recount now to my mother. "But continue with your story, aiti!"

"The next day was sunny and warm, and we left by train to Turku. Inna Pyykonen joined us at this point, along with her sister.

"At the time, there was an area between Helsinki and Turku called 'Porkkalan alue' – an area that was taken by the Russians after the war. The Finnish train went through this area, and when this zone came, the train stopped. In came Russian military men, with guns. My heart stood still. But all they came to do was pull down all the blinds on the windows as no one was allowed to see out in this territory. Actually, Aunt Eetti (surname Teegert) had a beautiful mansion in this area, in the Kirkkonummen area and it was confiscated. When the family finally got it back, what horrible shape it was in. Finland did get the area back after a few years, as I recall.

"So we got to Turku, and then boarded the ship. Marjut had a bottle, and I asked that her milk be boiled, but I am sure that they didn't boil it. Henry Malinen had given me some medicine, in case Marjut got sick, as is often the case with babies travelling.

"Dear Alfred was getting ready to meet us, in Sweden..."

Father continues now: "Finally the arrangements were made. I clearly remember that June day when I went to meet Maire at the harbour. Believe it or not, I was nervous! We had been separated for almost six months. At last, there they were: Maire and Jyri and the baby. I ran over to meet my family, but I felt that Maire was cool towards me. She did not give me a kiss, just handed the little baby to me. No, she didn't tell me how wonderful it was to see me, her dear husband."

"Well, I wasn't about to do that in public," says Mother. "But Inna came and hugged me, exclaiming how wonderful it was to see me again! Hugs and kisses there!" adds Father.

"Yes, well, she was Karjalainen and outgoing. Not like me, kind of shy, from Hamina."

Mother adds, "What I remember is that you asked me if I'd like some candy. You bought me a big bag full, and I ate them all on the train."

Now Father smiles and says, "Oh well, you sure had a great life!"

Truthfully, knowing my mother as I do, I could surmise how she was acting, almost miffed. She must have had mixed feelings about everything, and surely a touch of resentment because her husband had missed so much in the six months of separation. Of course this was not his fault, but all the same, there were misgivings, perhaps even jealousy or distrust on Mother's part. So, I could see her giving poor Alfred the cold shoulder. Once again, life was in turmoil.

But Mother continues: "I had forgotten my Swedish that I had once learned in school. We spoke in German to the Swedes. But quickly I learned Swedish, listened and read. We lived with Dr. Laansoo and his family. Everything seemed unreal; I felt lost. I cried a lot for Finland and my family. It was in reality very hard. The place where we lived with the Laansoos was a dwelling for doctors and nurses only. We lived here from June until September.

"After we arrived, Marjut got quite sick and I used the medicine Henry had given me. It worked.

"Tiiu and Kristi, the Laansoo daughters, helped to look after Jyri and Marjut sometimes. It was also nice to be able to speak in broken Estonian with the many friends that Alfred had already made in Tranos. Then we got our own little place on Sturgarten 5.

"The Swedish people helped immeasurably. Even our furniture was given to us by a man who owned the furniture store. When winter came we really didn't have clothing, but people arrived with clothes as well. I got a lovely winter coat. I treasured it.

"In the autumn, we had our first visitor from Finland: Tellervo Ojanen. Then Kerttu came with Elli Eerola. Kerttu brought some of our things with her and also some books. However, two of the books were confiscated. Even Helju, Fredi's sister, came from Denmark.

"The people who owned the house where we lived on Sturgarten had been living in America. They were American Swedes. They lived upstairs in their huge quarters there. Well, when they argued, they did so in English!

"New Year's Eve 1949 we could celebrate, finally, together. What a change from the previous year, when Alfred had been in hiding in Helsinki.

"Our place was set up very nicely. It had a big kitchen and then one other room. We had a pull-out sofa in the living area. The children had their own nice beds in a corner, which was separated by a bookcase. Plants were hung on the shelves as well. You know how I like to make a pretty home, yes.

We got together – a lot with friends, and one night we remember well. The Leithammers came to visit. This must have been about April 1949, as Marjut was just over a year old. They always brought chocolate for the children. Well, the children were delighted to get these treats, and soon I put them to bed. Later in the evening, I checked them to see that their blankets were on. I looked in on Marjut – she had not finished her chocolate; there were little round balls left. I picked one up, put it into my mouth and bit. Oh! It was such a chocolate that I have never since tasted! Marjut had been constipated, but these had slipped out of her diapers. Oh!"

Father enjoys this: "Yes, Maire got recycled chocolate! She ran out of the corner, "Ui, ui, ui..." She went straight to the sink, washing her mouth out, spitting. How we all laughed. Hey, you smelled for many months, Maire!"

"I did not, but boy, your fun lasted quite some time on my account!

"Well, Fredy painted a lot. Every weekend he painted, as he worked at the factory all week. It seemed that every Saturday Fredy needed some more paint and I was sent to buy it: ultramarine blue, cobalt blue, white. When I walked into the store, the owner knew exactly what I was coming for and for what colours. There are many paintings in Tranos done by Alfred.

"Two art exhibitions were arranged in Tranos of Fredi's works. The first one was in 1950, and Father sold many paintings. The Swedes understood and treasured art.

"We had very nice Swedish friends, the Rosenthaals and Mindis. Ella Rosenthaal was such a lovely lady. She cared for Marjut a lot, holding her when she visited. She taught me to sew and then – Fredi, how did I get my sewing machine? I don't know now, but I started to sew a lot. Jyri and Marjut were made beautiful matching clothes. I also learned to knit, getting patterns from Finland. I still have the blue and white knit dress I made Marjut, and the sweater that was heart patterned. I knit each child matching sweaters, pants and hats. How adorable they looked, as they walked with their father along the snowy streets in winter. The newspapers printed a story about the Estonian-born artist, and took a picture of the artist with his son. There they were, grinning into the lens. I still have the newspaper clipping but it has paled with age and is almost torn.

"In the fall of 1950 I had an ectopic pregnancy, which was quite a serious situation, especially then. I was sent to hospital quite far, and spent over three weeks there."

Mother doesn't tell me more, but I found old letters Father wrote during this time – they are quite disturbing. Was there more to the story?

Tranos, Saturday

Dear little Maire!

I have fussed all day so that I would have everything done by evening. I went shopping and tried to bake for the first time in my life! I have to admit that it didn't work out well, as I forgot to buy the yeast. I realized this after mixing everything together and the dough did not rise. The apple pie is of eating standard, but not the pulla. I am absolutely crushed by this!

I bathed and fed the kiddies ("muksut"). Now the little ones are sleeping. Every night, Marjut must have her prayer, "Let me rest by You," and we all pray that our little mother will soon be home, healthy and happy. We miss you!

I called you yesterday; I hope you got the message. I also got your postcard. Thanks. I hope you got my letter and the ten krons. I shall send again – now buy yourself some oranges and other things you need. I went to see Grunstrom. He wasn't interested in buying the painting and didn't even mention the money. But we'll manage, even though this world has a lot of people who are unfair.

I am writing in the kitchen, and thought I'd go and put this in the post, but I'll write tomorrow. Also, Marjut is not sleeping well as she slept in the afternoon. The faucet is dripping – I'll go and tighten it. There! Tomorrow I'll write more, hoping to be a little brighter.

Good night my dear!

Sunday:

The usual wake-up, as always: "Pee is coming!" I feed the children, do the dishes, get Jyri out to play. At noon Clary and Greetta came and invited us for dinner.

Jyri gladly went right away with Clary, and Marjut and I went later. The children had fun, as they watched all the cars go by from the window. We also called you. We were told that you are much better, so now my heart is at peace as I know how you are.

I miss you, even though at times I have been mean to you, but you understand, life has also not been easy for me. Life is so tiring at the factory, as I do not see anything brighter in the future. But now when you come home, dear, let's try to be understanding of one another. When everywhere there is misery, somewhere there has to be something better – at least our understanding for each other. If I am tired and miserable, then you, dear, should be in a happy mood. Don't start arguing with me, as then there is only empty wind that we go on about, and rude accusations. Understanding between us is the main thing. I promise at least to try to be more peaceful and less distressed. Don't think I love you less than before – if anything, I love you more.... this is true, real love.

Good night, Maire dear!
Your Fredy.
Now the children are sleeping so I'll take this to the mailbox.

Monday at home

My own dear love!
Yesterday when I phoned, I got the news that the surgery was done. This was a surprise to me as well as to Arnold (Dr. Laansoo). He said, though, that it's a lot cleaner and less dangerous to do it that way. It only takes more time for the healing of the incision. It is easier than an appendectomy.

The main thing is that everything goes well and you get home soon. My heart aches for you the whole time and home without you is so empty, cold. The children are doing nicely, eating well. Jyri is outside almost all day and Heljo is out twice during the day. Her appetite is better. Jyri went to the fair, and rode on the carousel. At times he says, "Mommy went for a car ride!"

On Saturday I had much work to do all day and I have to say it is hard to look after everything, get the place clean, as well as look after the children. I give you praise for the work that you do here and will remember in the future to give credit to you for your job.

On Saturday night we were at the Toomsalus and played cards until 2 a.m. On Sunday I took sun in the backyard, near the clothesline and the children played with their cars. Kristi and Tiiu called at lunch, and stayed. At 3 p.m. Juri and I went to eat and we got back a little after 4 p.m. I made Heljo food, as the little one slept the whole time that we were gone. After she ate we all left to go out again, and returned at about 7:30 p.m. I put the children to sleep, and they fell asleep immediately, dreaming sweet dreams. I went to the Laansoos to phone you. (Don't think anything's wrong!!!) I came home, thought of you, and then read the paper until midnight.

And today has gone, like all the other days, only every moment my thoughts are with you. As I write, Heljo is singing "laa, laa, la!" Jyri is playing with his friends outside, just under the window.

Tonight I have to paint once I get the children to sleep! I have to get some money so we will manage the three weeks. When you get home, we'll get a home nurse – that won't cost much, as you, beloved, have to get well.

Keep well and don't worry about us. I am already

used to housework. May God help so that you get well and come home! From my heart, my love,

Your Alfred

Little Heljo's letter!--**!))--= (scribble)
"Mother come home!" Little Marjut

The weeks went by and Alfred managed, though he had taken time off work. In those days, one did not get paid for missed work. Another letter was written, of which the last page is readable:

...You know, Maire, that I have done my best; we have to draw a line somewhere. I don't want to be blasphemous but I can't pray ceaselessly. I am humbled by this experience and, as I've said, before I know your thoughts and feelings – and this is not easy for me!
Why haven't you written? I have been waiting, and have come home at lunch to check for a letter, but no.

God help us!
Alfred.

I don't have the strength to write anymore.

Maire must have sent a loving (or forgiving?) letter, as the following correspondence is much more optimistic:

At home, Tranos

My own dear Maire!
Heartfelt thanks for your lovely letter. I am happy

that I have you as my wife. You have suffered much because of me and I can't make it up, except with my eternal love. I love you.

I haven't loved anyone in this world as I love you, though I have not really been able to show this to you, as I should have. I have been faithful to you and always will be.

Again there is a new road in our lives and God has led us to it. He punishes us and also gives us a chance to start again. We must walk this road and happiness can be ours as long as we have understanding and love between us. I ask you to understand these lines that I have written, my dear wife.

I am so incredibly lonely for you that it is difficult to sit and think. I just have to do something so that the time goes quickly.

Tomorrow I'll send you some more money so that you make out well. Don't be worried about me, I'll make out fine as long as you, my dearest, are well and recuperate fast.

I am needed at work, as there is a lot to do there. I promised to try to go to work on Monday. I'll try to get a nurse for the week; you can command from bed, you "little commandant"!

The children are well; their appetites are good. I have painted a little and also sold a little, so we are getting on fine. Nothing big, just some watercolours.

I don't think you will have to pay more than 40-50 kr. but just in case, it is better to have a little more, so I send you the money.

Yours forever, "Isu" and the little ones. Plus a kiss!

P.S. Ask specifically when you will be able to come home.

"So Maire arrived home, was nursed back to health, and life continued for us. Things were not easy, though. I had commitments, a family to feed.

"In our life, it seemed that every time we really needed money, someone would buy a painting. As luck would have it, I was commissioned by a man to paint a portrait of his young daughter. From this painting, I got a sailboat! So it was off to the sea again!

"We were learning the Swedish language, enjoying our life in Tranos. Every year we renewed our visitors visa, and after five years we could have applied for Swedish citizenship."

Mother continues...

"Jyri was a caring older brother, and the children enjoyed their daily routine of playing outside and visiting. Well, our little miss was quite headstrong, right from the start, also very independent. Jyri would hold on to Marjut's wrist, his hand firmly clasped around so that she would not take off. Was Marjut trying to lead Jyri?

"Marjut had a blue playsuit, or jumper, it was very nice. She always wanted to go to the park to play; there was a great playground there. But the children had their own sandbox and toys in our little yard. One day Jyri ran in and said, 'I can't keep Marjut! She's gone!' Marjut had gone to the park. It was a long way off for a little girl. When we finally caught up to the little wanderer, there she was, in her blue jumper, enjoying herself in the park.

"One day again: no Marjut. It was lunch hour, twelve noon. There was a special market that day at the market square so there was a lot of traffic. Also, people rode their bikes home for lunch in those days. Cars were coming and going, and it was unusually busy.

"I ran out, and then I saw Marjut, heading in and out of all the traffic on Sturgarten, with her little blue playsuit on, her blond hair bobbing up and down. She was going off to the market. I caught up behind her, but was too frightened to call, as she might then not look where she was going, or run in another direction. I held my breath and followed as finally she made her way to the market, quite oblivious of any problem whatsoever. She checked things out at the market as I kept watching her, and then I caught her, and of course she was taken straight home.

"After that, we had a continual eye on her, and she didn't escape too many times after that.

"But one day, Jyri did something very dangerous. A train track bordered the town, not far from our place. There was a fence running along the track at a certain spot. Well, Jyri got through a small hole in the fence. It was broken at that spot, and then the two children were climbing up to the tracks. The train was coming. Luckily, a neighbour was bicycling along, saw the children and quickly got hold of them. This was very scary.

"There was a mini-golf course also in town. Jyri went there one day, opened up the main sprinkler. The whole place was like a swimming pool.

"Once, Fredy and I went to the movies, a short distance from our house. Ella Rosenthaal was to keep watch over the children. Her apartment was just across the hall from ours. Remember, we lived in the lower part of the big house. You children were sound asleep when we left, so Ella just had to peek in once in a while.

"After the movie, we walked home, and as we approached the house, we heard 'tramppa, tramppa trampaaa!' Loud squeals and chanting of 'tramppa.' We rushed in – and there were Jyri and Marjut! They had moved their beds together to the middle of the floor, tossed all the sheets off, and were bouncing up and down, up and down on the beds, having a great time, all red-faced and jubilant.

"Another time I left to go to the market and again asked Ella to keep an eye on the children. We had a wood-burning stove as well as an electric 'plate' or portable two-burner stove. Jyri knew how to put the electric burner on, and the two children were both burning paper on this as Ella came in just in time. There could have been a big fire.

"From fire to water, the children were constantly getting up to mischief. Once, they put the water taps on in the apartment, and the sink was overflowing. We couldn't get the faucet to turn off, so had to wait for the men to come home. We were afraid to tell our landlords. So when Ella's husband arrived and then Fredy, the men set to work fixing the faucet.

"Marjut also called all the men she met in stores, 'Father.'

"Haircutting was a dilemma. Jyri had to get his cut first, and he did so like a real little man, but Marjut kicked up such a fuss! We finally got her to sit down in the chair, and the barber placed a wooden board around her. Afterwards, the children got a toy.

"There were lovely shops in Tranos, especially on Sturgarten. Such a pretty town, with the Sommen Lake. We should go and visit it again, and see if Mr. Helberg is still alive. He has written us faithfully every year ever since we left, right up until 1995.

"Among our friends were the Toomsalus: Helmar, Erna and their little Krista. They left for Canada in 1950, as many Estonians were doing.

"We liked Sweden very much but, you see, the scare that Fredy and even the children could be deported from Sweden was the only reason we decided that we too should leave. Unfortunately, there had already been cases of people being sent back.

"For many Estonians in Sweden, Russia was still too close. I personally had no worry as I was Finnish, but when our friends started to urge us to leave, we started to take this seriously.

"Johannes Kunapuu was the man who talked Fredi into leaving. So we started to get our papers in order. We needed to get medicals and inoculations. Dr. Paulsen was a radiologist who was involved with the immigration check-ups. He was the one who found out that Marjut had a heart condition.

"Father organized an art show in March 1951. I was also quite involved with this. I went to see about renting the hall, had a meeting with the manager there. After we had talked, he started to laugh very hard. I was taken aback. Why was he laughing at me? He told me that he was sorry to laugh, but he had never in his life seen such an energetic woman. Yes, I packed the paintings, put them on the kick sled and off I went to the hall.

"This show was a great success. Just about every painting was sold. Dr. Paulsen arrived in Tranos, late for the art show, but bought one painting, and would have bought more, but none were left. He had seen Fredi's work before, and urged that we remain in Sweden. The talent! 'We can make Alfred well-known here in Sweden,' he said. The doctor went back to Stockholm, and then called us. 'I have checked things out, and want to arrange another show for Alfred here in Stockholm.' The calls went back and forth, but in the end, we told him that we didn't have enough time for another show, as Alfred would have to take the time to paint. The kind doctor was such a promoter of Alfred's work that he kept calling. In the end, we had already bought our tickets and didn't want to cancel them.

"Often we wonder if we would have stayed a little longer and had the show in Stockholm, what would have happened? We may never have left. Another thing we are certain about is that in Sweden, Father would have been able to support his family with just his painting. All his life he could have devoted to art. People in Sweden appreciated art and promoted it. Life in Sweden was very good, and we had wonderful friends and supporters.

"The decision to leave was difficult, and very painful. But freedom came first, the freedom from worrying about political repercussions. Alfred had gone through so much already and really didn't trust the situation at the time, even in Sweden.

"We knew nothing about Canada. The only thing we remember is that someone said that aboriginals lived there, their land taken, and that a lot of immigrants were arriving yearly. At the time, our options were to either go to Australia or Canada. Canada was closer.

"Once again, we were packing. This was very hard, as we really had a great life, full of promise, in Sweden. This move would take me an ocean away from my family in Finland.

Leaving Sweden, 1951

"We left Sweden in June 1951. The Laansoos took us to the train station, and we have a picture where we are waving goodbye, looking through the glass window of the train. Two little heads looking out, not knowing really where they were headed. Their parents smiling forced smiles for the camera. They too did not know really where they were headed! The Laansoos had become dear friends, and they too would follow us to Canada within a year.

"We travelled to Denmark and then to Bremen, Germany. We stayed the night in a hotel, but this place was very eerie; it was a horrible place. I got the feeling that Gestapo had been there. Ugh. The travel agent in Sweden, who was Estonian, pulled a fast one on many of us. We paid for first class tickets, yet got the worst. Many people wrote to the agent, trying to get reimbursed, but to no avail.

"In England, we boarded the ship, the *S.S. Colombia*, a Greek liner. Our trip lasted nearly two weeks. With us were the Kunnapuus. Marjut was not to be trusted so she was harnessed. She had a lovely outfit with matching hat that I had knit. She threw the hat into the ocean. My, the children were well dressed. I had made a lot of clothes for them so that they would have lots to wear for a few years once arriving in Canada.

"On June 14th, 1951, we landed in Quebec City. Here, the nuns greeted us kindly, asking us if we needed food or any help. We went to the immigration check, had our papers stamped, and there we were: landed immigrants.

"We continued on to Montreal and went to meet the Leithammers, Paul and Erika. We had never met them before, but Paul's brother we knew from Sweden, and he had given us the address. We got a taxi, and arrived that first day in Canada at the doorstep of the Leithammers. We knocked, hoping for a reply. To their surprise, the Leithammers received some company: two adults, two children and three big suitcases.

"These people took us in and helped us. Kunnapuu and Father were going to stay in Montreal. Both already had jobs. That was the plan. But I started looking for Finnish names in the phone book, and couldn't find many. I cried and cried for two weeks straight, wanting to go back to Sweden.

"What a feeling! So alone, really, and lost.

"Then I felt that we should go on to Toronto; at least we knew others there. So we took the train to Toronto with the Kunapuus. The Veidenbaums greeted us at the station.

"We took a taxi to Linda and Lutt Luide's place but they were not home, so we decided to go and eat at a restaurant around the Bloor-Bathurst area. The restaurant was very rundown. We didn't know what to order because we did not know what the words were. We decided on a ham sandwich. This was on white bread It was awful, like biting cotton. I had one bite and had to run to the washroom to spit it out. Also, everything was dirty and smelly, quite appalling.

"I must say that the European immigrants who arrived during this time built Canada. Ya."

Father adds, "When we arrived in Toronto, I felt very depressed and felt that I had made a very big mistake. What an ugly dirty city! Everything seemed so primitive. I had a horrible empty feeling.

"Why didn't we turn back? Well, it would have cost a lot to return; we would have had to make out new papers to get back. The paperwork seemed overwhelming at this point, especially when we didn't know any English. We also kept remembering why we had come here: safety. We were far away from the troubles of politics. But, there was not much in the way of art, theatre…"

"Well, the Luides found us a place to rent on Grace Avenue," continues Mother. "We had one room and a kitchen. The children slept on a wooden bed in the kitchen. The other room was only big enough for a simple steel bed and dresser. But the apartment was horrible and we had to pay sixteen dollars a week for that. It was highway rubbery. (Mother pronounces 'robbery' as 'rubbery.') This was in 1951. Imagine what kind of money that was! We lived here for three weeks. Fredi got a job right away at a picture frame place, called the Photo Studio."

"Yes," says Father. "I got that job and worked hard. Before I knew it I was made foreman. I made pretty good money. Was it $13.00 a week? Anyway, we even had money left over after all the bills were paid. Actually there was a job offer also in Newcastle, which I was to take. This was as a cabinet maker, but I never went there."

Adding to this, Mother continues: "Father was speaking a lot more English now, and he had great recommendation papers from Sweden. First, the owner of the shop asked Father if he would show him how he would mat and frame a picture. Of course, as Father had been doing this for many years, it was nothing. The English gentleman who owned the business always said 'Will you please do…' 'Will you please get this…' 'Will you please…' Father finally got fed up and had to tell him: 'My name is not "Will you" (Viljo) – it is Alfred!' Later they would laugh about this!

"Agnes Kunnapuu knew how to read English a little bit, and was searching in the newspapers for another place," remembers Mother. "We ended up renting on the top floor of a house on Major Street. We made our furniture out of orange crates. The first thing built was the bookcase. That is always the most important item. Then we made a table and shelves using the crates. I put material in front of some of the boxes and it looked kind of cozy. The owner of the house wanted to protect the wood floors, so believe it or not, there were newspapers covering the floors! This was awful in our eyes. Immediately I took the newspapers off and laid down my lovely Swedish rag rugs. Also, I put a nice curtain on the window of the front door.

"The owner came up one night, knocking on our door. He asked where our children were. I motioned to him that they were sleeping. He was amazed at how quiet and well behaved the children were. He never heard them. When the children spoke, it was in Swedish.

"When we left this apartment, the landlord was hoping that we would stay. I had quite the time getting the rugs from him – he insisted that they were his now!

"Our friends Viva and Uno had just bought a small bungalow on Runnymede Gardens, so we moved in with them. We shared the kitchen and had our own bedrooms while Uno and Viva used the living room and dining area. There was a small pond, called Catfish Pond, across the street. Later the street was renamed Coehill Drive when the city ran a road through the woods.

"Father decided to start his own business now and he told his boss that he was leaving. This was difficult because the man was very nice – he begged Father to stay on!

"So, Artistic Woodwork was started at the small bungalow – in the basement. Kunnapuu, Veidenbaum and Alfred started the business together. Kunnapuu knew business as he had been a banker in Estonia. Veidenbaum was a financial backer. He was an editor of *Meie Elu*, the Estonian paper printed in Toronto. Alfred was the artistic director, creator, designer and manufacturer.

"Also, in the house on Coehill Drive was the first meeting for the Estonian Credit Union, and many other meetings for businesses.

"Uno had a Morris car and he drove us to places. When the time came for our baby to be born, it was Uno who took me to the hospital. He was in real estate so he could be more flexible with his time. Anne was born on December 27th, the same year we arrived in this new country. Uno came to the hospital to see me, but Father was working. When Father arrived with Uno to pick us up, the nurses asked who Alfred was! We joked about that. Anne was shown around the hospital ward wearing her brand-new knitted outfit that I had knit for her. She was very cute!"

Father, as a young man, painting, Toronto, 1955

As Mother is speaking, my thoughts too enter in. I interject with my own memories of this time. When Anne was born, I admit that I was not amused. She took up my space and time, my hold, that little hold, that I had on my parents. The baby was awfully cute, smiling with her pudgy cheeks, rosy in the sunlight.

I did a very bad thing – I tried to sell her.

I went door to door offering a baby for sale. One lady said that I could have her dog, a big nasty looking German Sheppard! Jyri came behind me, saying we would keep the baby. The deal was nixed.

Secretly though, I loved that smiling and cute little sister. I was sure to see that no one would hurt her.

My attentions went to Uncle Uno. Where did you meet Uno, Father?

Uno was a very kind and gentle man. Playing his accordion, singing and joking, with his wavy brown hair falling to his eyes, he would always be special to me. Uno had eyes that twinkled. He had come from the same country as Father – Estonia. Viva was a pretty lady, and I envied her. She always wore black stockings, and in Finnish there is a saying "black stockinged," which also has a connotation for "jealous one." For some reason I felt very jealous of Viva, perhaps I did not want to share Uno with her! I must have been a strange four-year-old.

Then I started to help everywhere. I made the beds and did what I could with my ability. I would surely be noticed. I was here too!

Jyri and I flooded the floors once in that little house. We used toilet paper to try to clean it up. The paper rolled off the holder, weaving in waves along the wooden floors. Soaking up and then being soaked up. Viva laughed.

Mother would try to teach Viva to bake. I watched as Viva sat on the kitchen chair, holding the bowl in her lap, whisking the eggs for a long time as they changed from bright yellow and opaque to fluffy pale yellow, like an artist mixing colours. It looked so good, and we were always allowed to lick the bowl.

Once, when Viva had unexpected company, she did not have a dessert to offer, so Mother gave her a cake that she had baked. When Viva's guests asked her what she had put into the cake, she kept rushing into Mother's room, asking her, "What is in that cake?" Immigrants helping each other.

Father made us wonderful "kokel mokeli" to make us strong and healthy. He whipped up eggs – lots of them, using a wire whisk. Then he added a bit of sugar and oats. We loved this treat.

As ever, I was trying to please everyone. One night, Mother and

Father had gone out. A man came to visit them, so Viva told him to wait; Maire and Alfred would soon be home. I decided that I should try to make the man comfortable, and showed him all the things we had in the living room – the vases, paintings, some books. As head entertainer, I was running out of ideas, but then rushed into Mother and Father's room. Out I came. "See Mother's new bra!" I held up the new item, pink, for him to admire. Viva would tell me this story decades later. Decades later, I still loved that lady dearly.

We moved a few years later to another house, one which I did not like. I have bad memories of the place for some reason. The people frightened me. We lived upstairs and had to share a bathroom with the others.

Mother and I walked up a huge hill to my kindergarten class. It seemed barren except for the houses that hugged the hill: unfriendly-looking eyes of windows, watching. Mother took me in to meet the teacher. I was hiding behind Mother, not wanting to go to this dreary and dark place. Those other children looked so knowing. There was a boy in that class who tried to pull his boots on; they were very tight. I see him even now, tugging to get those boots on. The teacher tried to help. He died. Mother told me. Did he die because he was trying too hard to get those boots on? Snow boots.

I painted some pictures in silence in that room and did not smile. I wanted to go home, where Anne was. I could go and take care of her. I was good, wasn't I?

Mother picked me up after the ordeal and I would skip happily down the street, going down fast, down the hill.

We moved again, this time to Windermere Ave.

The landlady was another stranger to stay away from. She never smiled. Our apartment was upstairs, and we had to use her front door to go up. I eyed her kitchen, so perfect: grey linoleum tiles, grey vinyl-padded kitchen chairs, with smooth chrome legs, shining. The counter was long, clean, neat. There were some clear containers on the counter, which were filled with candies, all shapes and colours. The colours dazzled me. I would sneak in there, staring at those candies that were clearly tempting me through the glass.

Every day I would think of those marvellous colours and want to taste them too. Thou shalt not steal, thou shalt remember thy manners at all times. I resisted temptation. Jyri! Come and see these candies! We decided that we had to try one. The landlady worked, and would not be home for some time. The coast was clear. I climbed onto the counter, reached up and slid the jar closer to me, unscrewing the top. Reaching in, I took a few candies, giving one to Jyri. We stuck the treats right into our mouths. They were sweet and tasted like peppermint. Rushing to swallow the hard candy, in case Mother would catch us, we didn't enjoy the others as much as the first ones. I did feel guilty, but was sure that the landlady would not notice that a few were missing. I lived in constant fear of being found out, with the lady rushing up to tell Mother that she had a criminal for a daughter.

I had to pay for another sin though. The lady never smiled. We were taught to say hello politely, which we did. One day, I was fed up with the scornful look in the landlady's eyes. Not being able to control myself, I told her she was an onion-face. A few days went by, but then Mother told me that she had heard that I had called the sour-faced lady a bad name. I must apologize. This was dreadful. I had to get my courage up. Alas, my dignity was at stake. But the deed had to be done, so I walked downstairs, met the looming lady in her kitchen and told her that I was sorry. Finally I saw a smile and her hands reached over to that counter I knew so well. Here, have a candy, she said. Thank you.

When we moved to Davisville Avenue I was going into grade one. We lived on the main floor of the house, subletting the upper rooms. We had bunkbeds in the little dining room, and we loved to jump on the beds.

Our yard was closed in, with huge grapevines running along the sides. At the back, the garages faced out into a narrow laneway. We were not allowed to go out into the lane, but somehow, we seemed to be roaming around a lot. Like moles, children seeking dark places, we played underneath the porch, the triangular light slipping in between the trellised boards. We skipped a lot, up and down the pavement.

"Blue bells, cockle shells, evi ivy over..." Anne tried to hold the rope in her little hand. Turn, turn! "Apples peaches pears and plums, tell me when your birthday comes!" Our days were filled with games.

But in school there was a sense of being outcast. I was not allowed to participate in gym because of a heart condition. Sitting on the sidelines, I felt lost, alone and frightened. So, five years later, when I was allowed to do sports, this became my obsession. Now that I think of it, somehow this paralleled Father's own time when he was sick and weak. But I digress again.

Family on a picnic, 1957 (l-r) Marjut, Jyri, Maire, Anne, Alfred

Adult lives were different:

"Father was busy with the business as it grew. Having moved out of the basement on Coehill Drive, the business was run in a factory space the men rented nearby. Kunnapuu left to go into banking, and

Father got a new partner, Mr. V—, whom he taught. There is something here that we do not know – but there were some underhanded things happening, and when Father found out, he sold out and left."

Mother wants to say more about this but won't. There is no point. Mother goes on: "Right away, Fredi got a job at Oxford Picture Frames. The doors were open everywhere for Father, as he was so good at designing. His dream was to bring modern picture framing to Canada."

"In hindsight, and in truth, there were to be many times that others would turn against Father. There were those who desired more money and more power. This was not Father's world. He really was an artist and excelled in the art that he produced – paintings or picture frame designs.

"At this time, Father also was involved with the Colour and Form Society, along with his friend Paavo Airola. They were some of the originals in that group. You know, someone wanted to represent Father, be his agent. He had seen Father's work at Hart House. He told Father that he would just have to paint; he would look after sales. The man's name was Avery Zacks. Father did not do this, which is another incredible twist of fate. Had Father gone with him, Father could have only painted, which is what he wanted to do! Why not let Mr. Zacks be his agent? Father's answer was complicated. He did not really understand the details; his English was poor; he did not trust anyone after all that he had been through; and he also feared that he would be told what kinds of paintings to paint, what would sell, etc. He wanted complete freedom in this regard. Somehow, Father felt that he could be boxed in. In hindsight, what a bad mistake!

"The route travelled was much more difficult, and freedom to paint was limited sheerly due to not having time for it! Business concerns always ate up energy and time." Mother sighs.

As a young girl, I can't remember much of Father. He came home late, was quite involved with Estonian artists and Estonian theatre in Toronto.

Often, in the summer, Father would leave for a few weeks to go and paint with his friend Abel Lee. As Father packed our Dodge, we watched: tent, folding chair, containers and sheets, paints, brushes, papers. When the car left, we waved as a cloud of dry dust sprinkled the laneway.

When Father returned, he had painted some more. We saw the colours and shapes, the flowing brushstrokes on canvases: images of where Father had been, Algonquin Park.

Abel and Father joked and laughed a lot. It must have been a wonderful respite from the demands of the city and, perhaps, from the realization that this new country was not what they had expected at all.

The story was told about how the two cavaliers had spent an unforgettable night at a fine restaurant in Quebec somewhere.

It had been rather late when the two dishevelled artists walked in. They had not shaved, their fingernails were dirty with paint. Seated at a lovely table, the two men proceeded to order dinner. Abel left to go to the men's room, and then Father told the waiter that, in reality, the man who just left the table was a recluse, an eccentric millionaire, who liked to go drawing as a pastime. Father was his chauffeur, and he would be pleased if the waiter and the rest of the staff would treat Abel well. Sitting down again, Abel was surprised when suddenly the room was astir with movement.

Waving hands, fluttering napkins, anything you like, sir, yes indeed, sir!

Father played along, enjoying the attention that he too received. He shortly confessed to Abel and it was hard to keep a straight face during dinner. Paying the bill, the artists left a tiny tip, did not turn to see the disappointed looks on the waiters' faces. Bursting into the night, the two artists held their stomachs, laughing and joking.

Well, the friends also had pitched their tent late in the night in a park. Getting up in the morning they realized that they had slept on someone's grave – this was a graveyard! Jokes were told about the restful sleep that Abel and Alfred had that night!

Two young men still pursuing their dreams to paint.

I saw the paintings on the walls and knew Father had exhibitions.

Those paintings really did not catch my attention, however, as they were a part of my life. Walls should be filled with colour, framed works of art, shouldn't they?

Occasionally I would hear the many Estonian friends speak about other times.

But what was it that always made me feel that someone was missing?

At dinner table, I would constantly count – one, two, three, four, five…but somehow the addition was not right. Should we not have had six at table?

Much later, of course, I understood…

Mother continues:

"My first job in Canada! I took over the job of a friend, who was a short-order cook, two nights a week. This was at Anderson's Milk Bar in Toronto.

"We wanted to buy our own house, so we needed to save money. In October 1956, for $16,000.00 we bought a bungalow in Richmond Hill. Why there? We wanted to get out of the city and into cleaner air, closer to nature. We had nice English neighbours, the Kenyons. My, the New Year's Eve parties! One of those nights, Father and Mr. Kenyon had quite a bit to drink. Father told his friend (also Fred) that he would ensure he got safely home across the street. Off they went. Father got to Fred's house, which of course meant another toast to the New Year, and then Fred walked our father home. Again, more salutes for the coming year. Father took Fred's arm, and took him home again. Finally, Father took off himself.

"Well, years later we heard what happened. Father, tipsy and walking a little wayward, arrived at the door. He pounded, wondering why I had locked the door. Finally, a tall lady with flowing brown hair answered the door. Father looked up and said 'Hey, you don't look like Maire!' He had gone to our neighbours, the McGregors, by mistake.

"We had fun. We were not rich; we were actually counting our pennies. But we always had company and enjoyed the fun with other Estonian artists and actors.

"I still had my job at Anderson's Milk Bar in Toronto. This was at Bathurst Street and Queen Street. I just remember always running a lot.

"So much work to do. I worked a lot of nights and so Father would take the children in the car and pick me up at the bus stop. There was no bus service into our area. The buses ran on Yonge Street every 45 minutes then. But the traffic was nothing compared to what it is today, just the distance was far.

"One day, in July of 1959, I had been rushing a lot. We had company, and I admit I wanted everything clean and tidy with all the baking and cooking done right.

"Going to work, I ran from the subway to get the streetcar. Running into the streetcar I felt a sudden pain in my chest. I fainted. I was helped up, and then went to see our friend, Dr. Barrett. No, I didn't go to the hospital. I went home but a few days later I ended up in the hospital for two weeks. It was a heart attack. That was it for working downtown."

…And, Mother, do you know how this affected me, as an eleven-year-old? I blamed myself for your heart attack. I sat by the ditch in front of our house with my friend Betty. I told her that it was my fault that Mother was sick. I must do more work, help out more. I was terrified of losing you! So it was, I did do more. I became that head caretaker.

Yes, aiti, continue now!

"So, in 1960, I got a job at the G.E.M. store on Yonge Street just north of Steeles. After three weeks on the job, I was called into the office. I was afraid that I was going to be fired. My English was not good. But I got a 10¢ raise! The boss told me not to tell anyone about it. I also was in charge of a department then. But the clientele came to me. I got a gold watch too. I'm not bragging but it's true.

"But there was a very unkind person who worked there and she treated others badly. I did not like this and wanted to leave. When I gave my resignation, the boss begged me to stay. But I wanted to leave.

"I worked at a bank at Drewry and Yonge Street then. But I didn't enjoy this work, so I started to apply to different places. I was accepted at Hydro, Zellers, but took the job at Sayvette Department Store at Steeles and Yonge Street. There I worked for nine years, moving up. Twice I was awarded 'Best Employee.' By this time I was not homesick for Sweden any more. Our life was here in Canada. Truthfully, we didn't want many to know where we had gone; we were somehow still afraid of the Communists. There were spies even here in Canada. Estonians just tried to get over it all, living here.

"We were happy to be a part of Canadian life now, and we also wanted to become Canadian citizens. So in October 1961 we officially became Canadians.* We were no longer strangers in a strange land. We were Canadians and proud of it.

"In 1961, Father again wanted his own business so he started Multiframe in Richmond Hill. This was a good business. Kunnapuu and Veidenbaum again joined Father in this enterprise. But Father was too naïve with some people, and he took in some other partners who ended up surprising him. This part will also not be told: lies and innuendos, and even a family and its ties almost broken. This was a major blow and left Father terribly broken.

"But actually, all along, Father only wanted to paint.

"In 1983, finally, we got our freedom! We sold our house; we were happy as birds. Our trailer had a flat tire as we just laughed and headed out to live at the cottage.

"These were wonderful years. Paints and nature. For sixteen years, we had a good life by the lake. We did not just sit down there, we went to theatre, concerts. We got involved with people in Picton, travelled. When Father had an art show, this money was used for our travelling account.

"We had a great and wonderful surprise when we had our fiftieth wedding anniversary. Marjut and Tapani organized something very

*from speech by Marjut, chapter 8, "Canadians" published by Clarke, Irwin and Company Limited 1965 "In Your Own Words" Nathan Davison and Eleanor Robertson

special for us in Hamina, Finland.

"We were supposed to go out for dinner with my sister Kerttu, but en route, we stopped to see the old church where we were married. We were escorted to the church, thinking there was some christening going on because we heard some music. I turned to leave, but my sister Tuula and her husband Kari pushed us forward – and then it was like a dream. I saw Marjut coming down the aisle with flowers; I saw Tapani in the corner, friends from long ago. We got to the altar and there was a pastor there. Before we knew it, we were repeating our wedding vows! Alfred repeated 'I do' again, in front of some of the people who had been at our humble wedding during the war.

"It was truly something. We had a reception afterwards at the Officer's Mess, an elegant place. Some members of the Hamina Male Choir sang at the service and reception. (Alfred sang in that choir 50 years ago!) A special song was sung."

Returning

> Though all my travels have led me far
> from the birthplace of long ago,
> blue and white flags of familiar places,
> lead me: lead me, to the place I know.
>
> Warm are the feelings that stir my heart
> blue and white flags wave in the sky:
> bring me to rest in familiar places
> (Spinning and spinning of spaces)
> as time, as time of my life goes by.
>
> Life holds its secrets for you and I
> leaves that keep changing every day:,
> homeward towards the familiar places
> (Spinning and spinning of spaces)
> it's where, it's where in my heart I'll stay.

Lightness and darkness for everyone,
circles completing in each life.
Bring us to rest in familiar spaces,
(Spinning and spinning of spaces)
as time, as time takes us home again.

(Music and lyrics, Marjut)

"What a day! A tremendous gift for isi and me. When we left the reception late that night, followed by relatives and friends, we heard a tremendous clunking behind the car. How we laughed! Katrina had tied huge cans to the rear bumper and they were making quite the concert behind us – the loud clinking and clanking was a great end to a wonderful day. The cans were heavy, not light as newlyweds often have. Ours were mellowed with age, and heavy with history! We bounced along.

"That whole summer was exciting because we were also in Estonia for the remembrance of the Estonian soldiers. This big event was in Tallinn, where hundreds of men and women gathered from around the world to share and remember the times spent in that very different and difficult time of Estonia's history, which we linked with that of Finland. The 'Soome Poisid' ('Finnish Boys') were reunited.

"Father was asked to do a granite memorial, which was unveiled at Kaarli Kirik, Tallinn's biggest church. It was a big honour and the church was packed. Paul Saar, our dear friend, led in the service that important day. Alfred's gift back to his own country was a touching one. It is on the wall in that church.

"While we visited Finland, we were also re-acquainted with lost friends Oke Jokinen, the Paavolas, Maire Poyhonen, and the man who risked so much for our freedom – that "brother" of Alfred's, Pentti Taavitsainen. We didn't think that anyone had really changed. Pentti was still the same freedom fighter and generous human being.

"Father said to me 'I'm not rich, but I am rich.' Father loved to putter around. He built an addition to the cottage and a studio. Little

171

grandchildren grew up. We had a lot of company all the time. Many people have sat around our kitchen table, a great oval table, always set nicely with Finnish tablecloths and flowers. The conversations at the table usually turned to art and music. Our home was cozy and paintings hung everywhere. Father's pants all seemed to have paint on them, too!

"Funny how it is the little things we remember! Now look at you, Marjut, the same as Father – your pants have paint on them too! You used to get angry when Father got paint on his clothes when he went to work in the studio! Brand new pants were especially susceptible to paint.

"What a love for joking Father had! He loved to laugh, took great pleasure from the smallest things. Anne recalls Father buying a new hat shortly before he died. He was in the store and 'modelled' the hat, carrying on in his happy way. Taking a few exaggerated dance steps, looking in the mirror, Father had a great time. This was a simple hat, but why not make it an exceptional hat? Why can't we learn from this? Take the simplest things and make them special.

"How Father loved nature! Every day the birds, the greens in the trees, the shimmer of the lake were noted. Father walked every day with the dog down the lane, swinging his arms, stopping to look at a certain view, a certain field or tree. His artist's eye always took in the beauty around him." Mother's voice trails off.

I watched my father and saw that he was getting older. But he was full of life, ideas, spirit, wisdom and kindness. He was embarking on a new series of works, bigger in size. The clock was ticking by the kitchen stove, and soon Father was going to be eighty. The time was running out and of course we did not know this.

Mother continues: "Father never complained about his health, and he was always more concerned about me. I did notice he was at times very quiet and introspective. Mostly, he wanted to take life in a happy way, not be upset or worry about things. This was not easy to do; we did have a lot to worry about. But anyway, we had a good life those years at the cottage. Father kept painting and he had a lot to paint. As if he sensed that something was wrong, he kept telling me where to put the paintings, and also, he said he needed to finish one piece, which shows prisoners in chains.

"But one day all this ended and now here I am alone sitting at the cottage.

"But I have Father's paintings around me; I have him here in spirit all the time."

Mother's life is not easy, we know this. Her eyesight is failing, she lives alone with her little dog. She will not abandon Father's memory. She is at the window. She has her Alfred there.

Alfred's 80th birthday, June 1999. (l-r) Marjut, Jyri, Maire, Anne, Alfred

Now the new calendar has been put up, a year of new beginnings: 2003. We finally have an art show of Father's works in Toronto. What a shock. Why? I never really understood nor saw just how great an artist my father was. The gallery was full of paintings from the 1940s to 1999. A huge crowd, a big success. The colour! Alfred was truly a genius with his use of colour. His sensitive and thought-out compositions keep speaking to many viewers. His treatment of landscape is a thing of beauty.

One artist called me a day after attending the show and stated that Alfred's colours are wonderful, and they are friendly colours. I was taken aback. He asked if Father was friendly himself. I said, yes, he surely was! I put the receiver down and looked at the paintings we have on our walls. Why had I not noticed this myself? These paintings are so very close to me.

Yes, of course! The colours are truly friendly. Here are strokes of a gifted, gentle artist. One who never bragged about his work, never marketed his work.

Oh, to have Mr. Zacks here now!

Will it be true that one has to market one's artwork all one's life? Or can the work stand out, timeless and always full of life? True, true, the audience must come.

I went looking for my father. Suitcase, paints, papers, steadfast, to Haapasaari, Finland.

This is where Father and I were to go to paint some day. This is where I knew I had to make the journey. Father, where are you? Your memory is in the shadows; it moves like the wind and changes shapes. Swept shadows on the rocks, holding such colour! Hues of blues, pinks, greens, yellows on the smoothly-formed rocks. What history! I cling to the rocks and feel grounded, timeless. Birds sweep food away as clouds form. I do not find my father. But what was his message? Disoriented, I sit up. Things are not as they appear.

My soul soars towards something majestic and magical.
Thank you, isi.

Alfred Karu's oil painting: Lapland, Finland, *from a trip there in 1988*

A Day in Viljandi

Bright was the Sunday that we spent together
exchanging our histories in one day.
Warm was the time when we walked through the old
streets
recounting the history of our past.
Moments remembered with fragments blue in haze.
Who were these people who built a country
suddenly caught as the pawns of war?
Books black and white could not tell the tale.
Silences spoken, history spoken -
Freedom speaks!
Who knew then what our future held.

Time, it stood still, then, while we were together
searching for lifelines no longer there.
Time, was it gentle as we spent each moment
uncertain of when we would meet again?
Tangible, fragile our happiness now shared.
At the old house now filled with our laughter
together now, as if in a dream.
Footsteps now dancing the day was gone.
Flags that were waving, nation reclaiming –
Freedom speaks!
Never to walk that path again.

Music and lyrics: Marjut Karu

Printed in the United States
28011LVS00001B/259-303